Praise for *God's Dictio...*

"The way we use, interpret, and understand words shapes our experience of the world. Words can lead us to deep suffering or help deliver us to joy and enlightenment. In *God's Dictionary,* Susan Corso gives us a divine glimpse into the origin of words and presents us with a truly spiritual perspective. Drawing from a wide range of material, as well as from personal experience and knowledge, Corso's book reads like a spiritual text—it delivers insight, understanding, and ultimately a context in which to transform our inner and outer worlds."

—JONATHAN STAR, author of *Rumi: In the Arms of the Beloved*

"Somebody needed to write this book—to show how, for better or worse, words are psychospiritual time bombs. In her easygoing, conversational style, Corso conducts a tour of loaded words, pointing out the ways we use them to close ourselves off from enlightenment or open ourselves to it."

—DEAN SLUYTER, author of *The Zen Commandments*

"Susan Corso has given us a sparkling exploration of the spirit infused in our words . . . and our lives."

—STEVEN HARRISON, author of *Doing Nothing*

God's Dictionary illuminates and delights spiritual seekers and word lovers alike. Susan Corso's sacred etymology is both whimsical and inspired; playful, delightful and profound.

—CHRISTIAN DE LA HUERTA, author, *Coming Out Spiritually*

God's Dictionary

God's Dictionary

Divine Definitions

for Everyday

Enlightenment

Susan Corso

JEREMY P. TARCHER/PUTNAM

a member of Penguin Putnam Inc.

New York

Most Tarcher/Putnam books are available at special quantity discounts for bulk purchase for sales promotions, premiums, fund-raising, and educational needs. Special books or book excerpts also can be created to fit specific needs. For details, write Putnam Special Markets, 375 Hudson Street, New York, NY 10014.

Jeremy P. Tarcher/Putnam
a member of
Penguin Putnam Inc.
375 Hudson Street
New York, NY 10014
www.penguinputnam.com

Library of Congress Cataloging-in-Publication Data

Corso, Susan.
   God's dictionary : divine definitions for everyday
   enlightenment / Susan Corso.
      p.   cm.
   ISBN 1-58542-169-3
      1. English language—Religious aspects—Meditations. I. Title.

   BL65.L2 .C76   2002
   200'.3—dc21   2001050766

Printed in the United States of America
10   9   8   7   6   5   4   3   2   1

BOOK DESIGN BY AMANDA DEWEY

This book is dedicated to
the best daughters of my heart,

Jacqueline and *Rona;*

the best word wizard,

Richard;

the best beloved,

Elinor;

and

the Deeper Magic in every Word.

Contents

God's Dictionary

Introduction

Words are powerful. The very means by which we communicate to ourselves and to others, words determine *how* we present ourselves in the world. The language we choose affects the quality of our lives. How vital it is to use words that are inspiring, uplifting, and empowering! If we want to live well, we have to find the language for a life well lived.

God's Dictionary is the spiritual take on everyday words. In it, I take the currency of common words and use spiritual etymology to make light shine from within each one. Let me tell you the story of how I came to write *God's Dictionary* . . .

All of the women in my family were wordsmiths. They did crossword puzzles and acrostics, made worse-than-terrible puns, and were lovers of any kind of wordplay. I asked for my very own dictionary for my fourth birthday because I was tired of being told to "look it up!" Then I read it cover to cover.

Lo and behold, I found that I, too, had a love of words. I also had a love of God, a love rooted deep within me. Life set me up as a spiritual counselor; people have been coming to see me for nearly twenty years to discover how to make their everyday lives better. Over the years, I have realized that part of my work is to be a spiritual word detective—searching for clues in the words that my clients use to describe who they are and what they want to be, to do, and to have.

In my counseling practice, I heard my clients use the same words over and over again to describe their experiences and their desires. Now, in a session I practically fly to the dictionary to find the deeper, spiritual meanings behind the everyday words they use. People feel deeply heard. More important, they receive illumination from their own words interpreted within a spiritual context. Change happens, in some cases, almost instantly. Toltec shaman don Miguel Ruiz writes, "The word is so powerful that one word can change a life. . . ." It can. It's happened for me, and it's happened for my clients for nearly twenty years.

Words. Everyday, plain, simple English words hold answers to our deepest questions. Surprised? Here is a personal example of how the spiritual take on words can heal:

One of the things my mother used to say when I was a child was, "I'm so disappointed in you." She said it often enough that my adult life was frequently tainted by disappointment, and for the longest time, I couldn't figure out why. One rainy day, I felt an urgent inner prompt to look up the word in the dictionary. Odd, I said to myself, for I knew what disappointment meant—or so I thought. I dragged Dr. Webster's *magnum opus* from the shelf and blew off the dust. Illumination awaited me.

Disappointment.
Dis-, as a prefix, means *not.*
To -*appoint* someone is *to choose* them.
Hence, when I feel disappointed, I am feeling *not chosen.*

I realized that it wasn't that others weren't choosing me, but that *I* wasn't choosing the things that were good for me! With that, my disappointing experiences waned and vanished.

You might be wondering why the title *God's Dictionary*. For us literary types, there's been a *Devil's Dictionary* since 1911. Isn't it about time God had one? That aside, the real reason is because I started to wonder about words and God. Actress/Impersonator Anna Deavere Smith has said, "I wanted to know what the way we use language tells us about who we are." I wanted to know it, too.

Without exception, every book we deem scripture, both Eastern and Western, has something to say about words. In the Christian Scriptures, the word is made flesh and dwells among us. In the Koran, a good word is like a good tree whose root is firmly fixed and whose top is in the sky. In the Talmud, God has no other words than human beings. In the Tao te Ching, true words aren't eloquent. I could go on and on. What is it, I asked, about God and words?

Follow my theological argument. God creates with words. According to the Hebrew Bible, humanity is made in the image and likeness of God, *ergo*, we create our lives with our words. Words are the single most important tool we have to create change.

Words arise from within us. The deepest, truest words come from Spirit, or what the rabbis of old called the Divine Spark. This is the whole, pure place of silent knowing inside you. The Divine Spark or Spirit gives rise to Soul. This is where mind and heart experience karma and lessons, and where our personalities and belief systems reside. Soul gives rise to Body. I look at it this way: Divine Spark is the ink, Soul is the paper, and Body is the envelope. All of them are equally important when you want to send a letter. And what's in a letter? Words.

You will be reminded throughout *God's Dictionary* that you have a choice about words every time you encounter them. You can choose how you use words. You can choose how you are affected by words. Your words belong to you. They are the information you give out to the world. Their meanings are yours to determine.

Each word in *God's Dictionary* begins with a spiritual etymology. Traditional etymology is the branch of linguistics that treats of the origin and history of words. *God's Dictionary* uses spiritual etymology—the branch of linguistics revealed to me that treats of the spiritual origin and history of words.

Then, there is a teaching story to demonstrate how the word works in living a practical spiritual life. Afterward, you find a *How* question that addresses the word in your life today. Finally, there is what I call an *Infinition*. This is a word I've coined, which is for the purpose of expanding how you incorporate the word in your life.

Happily, I quote Theodore M. Bernstein in *Miss Thistlebottom's Hobgoblins*, "The words speak for themselves. And that is what words are supposed to do."

Dr. Susan Corso
New York City
October 31, 2001

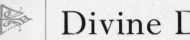 Divine Definitions

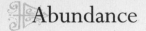Abundance

ab- = **from**
+
-unda = **wave**

Let's wade right into it, shall we? Money. We've all heard spiritual people talk about abundance issues or prosperity issues, and what they're really talking about—what we're all really talking about—is money. I learned the lesson of abundance the hard way—by being broke for a long time. Being broke, as movie mogul Mike Todd has said, is different from being poor; poor is a permanent state of mental affairs and broke is only temporary. How did I learn to be abundant? From the word itself.

Abundance happens in *waves*. It's cyclical. There are times when I have less (and some etymologists think the Middle English was *habundance* from the verb *to have*) and times when I have more. The secret to the waves is giving, totally unrelated to whether I have less or more. Abundance is an inner feeling of belonging in the cycle, of being part of something larger, something limitless. The easiest way to generate more is to give whatever you have. It doesn't matter if it's one dollar to a homeless person or clothes you haven't worn to a local charity! When you're feeling broke, give, and you'll remember that you do belong to the cycle of abundance. Ask: How can I give and start the waves of abundance flowing my way today?

Infinition:
I belong to the cycle of infinite abundance in the universe. As I give, the waves, which before seemed to be ebbing, now begin to flow like the tides of all the oceans.

Abuse

ab- = away
+
-ūti = to use

Abuse is almost an overused word today. Child abuse, domestic abuse, substance abuse are nothing new. They have always been around. We just didn't discuss them openly until the last twenty years or so. Why do we cross the line of use to abuse? What is it about human beings that makes us push the envelope of utility for nearly everything? We used nuclear energy very nearly to destroy a nation before we began to research radioactive isotopes as curative for cancer. Most everything and everyone around us has utility, but in utilizing these resources we must be wary of the fine line that separates use from abuse.

To abuse, as its Latin roots show, *uses away* resources. It pushes past usefulness to utilization, which is abusive. It's really a form of usury as we borrow or take what isn't ours, and it comes with high interest and penalties. Utilization of people creates abuse that is as hard on the abuser as it is on the one abused, especially if the abuser is never given the chance to change and heal. Abusers most often create abusers; it's rare for abusive behavior to arise spontaneously. As Oscar Hammerstein II wrote, "You've got to be taught to hate and fear." This is what causes usurious, abusive energy between people. Ask: How can I be sure to use things appropriately today?

Infinition:
I know how to use my resources appropriately. If abuse has been part of my life, I commit to healing now for my own sake and for the sake of all people touched by abuse.

Adoration

ad- = to
+
-ōrare = to speak

Traditional etymology would separate this word in Latin as *ad-* +*-ōrare*, or, to speak. Speaking is only partially how we adore someone or something. Spiritual etymology digs more deeply. What you adore— *a-* = (from) +*-dore*= (the gift)—is that onto which you project, and by extension give, your own *gifts*.

This is what happens when seekers align themselves with a healthy, genuine guru. I think the premier guru in the West is Jesus of Nazareth. When we adore Jesus, what He does is reflect our own true giftedness back to us. Despite our fears to the contrary, there is no creature on earth without its own particular gifts and abilities. That's right—not one. It's a matter of expanding your awareness to name your gifts truly.

Are you gentle? Patient? A good listener? Really efficient? Organized? Energetic? Good with animals? Children? Elders? Bring the divine gifts you have to everything. Ask: How can I give out of my own giftedness today?

Infinition:
My gifts are for the whole world. I give them freely out of adoration now, and am abundantly gifted in return.

Alone

al- = without
+
-onus = burden

This word has a surprising etymology given the ways it is used ordinarily, which are, of course, pejorative. Someone wise once wrote, "Loneliness is solitude made wrong." When a client of mine booked a ticket for a week's holiday in Paris, she was asked, "Are you going alone?" The tones she heard were a mixture of horror and fear—even pity. You can hear the subtext, "A holiday? Alone?" Why not?

One of the real meanings of alone is *without burden*, fancy-free, lacking cares. A rare pleasure! What a delight to go off to Paris for a week with no plan but to enjoy oneself! Indeed, all that's required to live a joyous and meaningful life is for one—your Self—to show up.

The spiritual etymologist adds a deeper meaning here: *All + One.* Drinking her cappuccino on the Rive Gauche, I know my friend is showing up as her Self, sporting a Mona Lisa smile and thinking right now that she's not alone or lonely for we are all one. Ask: How can I allow myself to be without burden today and see that we are all one?

Infinition:
When I am alone, I cast my burdens away lightly and enjoy my solitude. After all, we are all one.

Anger

angere = to strangle

also

angr = grief

Add just one letter to anger and you get *danger*. A lot of us feel danger when there's anger brewing either in others or in ourselves. The reason is that we are unsafe with our own anger and *ergo* unsafe with the anger of others. Anger itself is simply energy—neutral in nature—like electricity. Electricity can dry your hair or electrocute you; it depends upon how you use it. The same is true of anger.

The Latin etymology of the word means *to strangle*, and that's often how we feel when we're angry—either like we're being strangled or that we'd like to strangle someone else! Often, anger is a simple indicator that we need to say a clear *No* to whatever is causing the anger. I grew up believing that nice girls (and I was one—emphasis on the *was*) didn't get angry. It took years for me to get in touch with myself when I was angry. Once I did, I freed up a great deal of emotional energy for myself since I wasn't strangling it. I've also discovered that often deeper than my anger is sadness, so it's no surprise that the Old Norse word for anger means *grief*, is it? Related words to anger are telling as well: anguish, anxious, even angina.

Anger doesn't have to cause danger because we can always choose how we act on it. If we can allow it simply to be, anger can become a trusted friend in the sense that a seeing-eye dog is a friend to its blind owner. Anger is a guide worth our trust. Ask: How can I make choices about my anger (or that of others) today?

Infinition:
I trust my anger to guide me in my true path. It shows me when to say *No* to support myself. I am grateful for the power of anger.

Appreciate

ad- = to
+
-pretium = price

We all like to feel appreciated. Appreciation makes us feel valued. I had a meeting with a brilliant entrepreneur recently. He asked me to be a spiritual consultant on a merchandising project. I expressed interest, and then he asked me what my services would cost. I quoted him a price and explained how I got there. I explained that it was impossible actually to price or pay for what he was requiring of me, so all I could do was charge him for my time. To demonstrate, I asked how I could charge him for the dream that sent me the perfect image for his product. Wisdom is invaluable, and I traffic (most of the time) in spiritual wisdom.

Plenty of us have trouble with spiritual practitioners of any kind charging money for their services. We appreciate them, don't we? The Latin roots of appreciate mean *to price* or place a value on something. Since healers and the like work on invaluable levels of consciousness, we can at least show our appreciation by valuing the time they devote to us. Ask: How can I fairly appreciate someone's value today?

Infinition:
I know how to show my appreciation of the value for personal attention devoted to me.

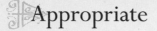Appropriate

ap- = to
+
-proprius = one's own

When we see or hear this word, most of us think of propriety in the Miss Manners or Emily Post sense. The word can also be a verb. Appropriate means *to take for one's own*. On the spiritual path, what we appropriate is vital to the quality of our lives. It's about ownership, plain and simple. What do you own in your life? Prosperity? Misery? Health? Worry? Although I am usually disinclined to approach things from the negative, ask yourself this: What are you disowning? When we say we're working on our "stuff," what we're referring to is the unconscious aspects of self that we aren't owning.

For years I actually disowned the notion of a healthy body. In fact, I pretty much disowned my body entirely. It's hard to take care of what we don't even acknowledge! I remember seeing a photograph of a woman's forearm in *The New York Times Magazine* one Sunday for an article about socially learned body image insanity; the caption read, "I remember the day I realized this was mine." That was the day I started to learn how to appropriate my own body appropriately. It turns out . . . I like it here. Ask: What do I need, or perhaps already have, that I can take for my own today?

Infinition:
I willingly own what's mine whether I've disowned it in the past or not. I appropriate what is appropriate for me.

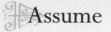Assume

ad- = to
+
sūmere = to take

from

sub- = under
+
-emere = to buy or redeem

There is a saying in Alcoholics Anonymous that when one assumes, one makes an ass out of you and me. The word itself tells us that to assume something is *to take* it upon ourselves. Indeed, when we assume something about another person, we place a burden upon them (in the guise of taking it on ourselves), be it to measure up to what we've assumed or to contradict it. Often the burden which comes with assumption is one of resentment.

When I assume that you will want the same thing you always have in a favorite restaurant, I take away your option to choose. The deeper etymology explains it better. When I make assumptions about you, I *buy (or sell) you right out from under yourself*. It is more effective for all human relating if, instead of assuming, we ask questions. Assuming eclipses the right to change our minds, one of the most singularly delightful aspects of being human. And whilst a dinner menu seems perhaps unimportant, apply the principle to raising children or buying a house! Furthermore, God gave us each one principal gift, that of free will. Its activity is choosing. Ask: How am I making assumptions about myself or people I love today?

Infinition:
I am forever free of assumptions about myself or others. I ask questions and discover the joy of choosing again and again.

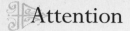Attention

ad- = to
+
-tendere = to stretch

I can still hear Mrs. Fogg, my first-grade teacher, interrupting my reverie that fall, "Pay attention!" I remember distinctly my six-year-old thought at the time, *What does it cost?* There is indeed a price for attention. Whenever I attend to one thing, it is to the exclusion of others. In truth, I can't be sitting at *Der Rosenkavalier* and *The Sound of Music* at the same time.

The root word for attention comes from the same word as *tendon* and it means, just as is the natural function of a tendon, *to stretch*. When I pay the price of attending, I stretch my conscious awareness toward that which I am choosing to attend, and, by default, I miss other things. Whilst it may sound as though I am missing out, how much more do I miss out by splitting my attention? Then I never get the full blessing of the price I pay.

Maharishi Mahesh Yogi is known for saying, "Do less, accomplish more." I'm pretty sure Mrs. Fogg wasn't a devotee of the Maharishi, but she was right! First grade was a lot more productive when I paid the price of paying attention. Ask: How can I truly stretch my attention to where I want it to be today?

Infinition:

I am happy to pay the price of attention. I attend to what I choose and everything in my stretch is a blessing.

Awareness

gewaer = cautious, on guard, taking care

or

a- = to
+
-warō = object of care

The Anglo-Saxon etymology of this word points to the sense of awareness as being fearful of something, of standing on guard against an unknown danger. It is the awareness we plead with our children to have as they cross the street for the first time on their own. There are, of course, times when this sort of wariness is warranted. Dark alleys at night come to mind. Using a spiritual definition of the word, awareness brings us a much greater gift. There is a saying in Alcoholics Anonymous, "If you can't see God, guess who turned away?"

Awareness—the sense of guarding what is valuable to us without fear—is what we can bring to much-desired wares or *objects of care*, things we want and choose. To be aware is to include the things we choose in our consciousness. Often, loving someone includes awareness of their daily schedule, so we know when we can connect. Or remembering to ask when someone we love has a scary doctor's appointment. Genuine awareness is a quality of love. Ask: How can I include the things I care about in my mind and heart today?

Infinition:
My awareness is limitless. I know what I need to include in it and what I need to let go right by. I am aware of God at all times.

Belief

be- = about
+
-lief = gladly, willingly

Old High German relates this word to the idea of love (think of the German for love, *liebe*), and in point of fact, we actually do love what we believe— whether it's positive or negative. Think of it: There are people who actually believe that the weather is a personal affront to themselves. Then there are those of us who slog out and sing in the rain. Belief is another one of those neutral things in life, like electricity. Its effect depends entirely upon how we choose to use it. We can believe in goodness or wickedness; it's simply a choice.

If we look at the word deeply, albeit with a Shakespearean twist, we'll see that belief is what we are *about gladly*. You'll hear, in *Romeo and Juliet*, a line from the Nurse, "There is a nobleman in town, one Paris . . . ; but she, good soul, had as lief see a toad . . . as see him." Today we might say, "I'd just as soon see a toad as see him!" Though Shakespeare uses lief in the sense of not wanting something, I'd as lief that we all remember that we have a choice as to where we put our belief. Ask: What am I about willingly today?

Infinition:

Wherever I have been willful in my life, that is where I can locate and willingly examine my beliefs. Likewise, I choose to place my belief only into that which makes me both willing and glad.

Belonging

be- = be

+

-langian = along with

Belonging is one half of the quintessential human dilemma. The other half is individuation. Much of our lives, we swing back and forth between these two extremes of survival needs. Interestingly, the roots of the word *along* tell us something about belonging. They mean both *from* and *against*. We want it, and are conflicted about it at the same time. Sound familiar? I played it out in high school classically. I wanted to act, and in the first show of our season, I was cast in a great role. There was no part for me in the second show of the semester, so they asked me to do costumes. I did them, but with little grace. The pendulum of wanting to belong had swung the other way. I wanted instead to individuate and be a star again.

The Anglo-Saxon roots imply an appropriate relationship to belonging. They mean *to be along with*, not to belong **to**. Here is how we belong. First, we belong with God, then we belong with ourselves, then we belong with others. When belonging comes with *to*, it borders on possession, and thereby annihilation. When we belong with, we are whole unto ourselves and we offer that wholeness for the good of all. Ask: How can I belong with others today?

Infinition:
I no longer belong to anyone or anything. Instead, I belong with the family of God here on earth. We are all individuals, whole and complete in ourselves, and we bless each other with our wholeness.

Betrayal

be- = about
+
-trādere = to deliver up

from

trans- = across
+
-dare = to give

This word summons the dissonant musical chords of the silent movie melodramas for me. Our hero or heroine is about to hear something decidedly unpleasant. Can you hear the pipe organ? Betrayal is about delivering up someone to something usually not very appealing, isn't it? Betrayal is actually a model for learning because without exception, it wakes (shall I say shakes? quakes?) the people involved to a deeper truth. Think deeply. Betrayal—that delivering up—is a universal human experience. Why do you suppose that is? It's because we learn deeply from betrayal, whatever its format.

The classic, archetypal betrayer is, of course, Judas Iscariot (properly, of Kerioth). We've all heard someone described as a Judas. Believe it or not, betrayal by another is the least painful kind. The deeper meaning of the word—*to give across*, meaning against—shows us that self-betrayal is the tenderest, most painful kind of all. It took me years to learn to say *No* in relationships because I wanted always to keep the peace. Simply put, when I say *Yes* and I need to say *No*, or when I say *No* and I need to say *Yes*, I give across/against myself, and I betray myself. Ask: How can I deliver for myself today?

Infinition:
Betrayal hurts, and despite this fact, I know that it always has a higher purpose, especially self-betrayal. I turn to the Spark of Divinity within me today and I let betrayal teach me.

Birth

gebyrde = **to bear**

Like death, birth is an obvious part of the process of being human. If you've ever birthed a child, or been present at the birth of one, you know the awe that it engenders, as well as the mess. Birth ain't always pretty, but it's always beautiful. This goes for babies just as much as symphonies, and selves. The Anglo-Saxon root of the word means *to bear*, and we all bear birthing pains and trauma regardless of what we're birthing.

The thing that intrigues me about birth relative to the spiritual life is that it's an ongoing process. Unlike babies, who are born once physically and it's over, the birthings of a soul take a whole lifetime. We bear ourselves as one thing until we get pregnant again with another part of ourselves, and then we give birth to that new aspect of self. The key is to remember that parts of us are always getting pregnant (and it matters not whether we're male or female), parts of us are in the gestation period, and parts of us are giving birth each and every day. Ask: How can I bear consciously what I'm birthing today?

Infinition:

I am the birther of my Self in all my aspects. I remember that I am in the process of bearing new and exciting parts of me all the time.

Blame

blasphemare = to speak ill of, revile, reproach

from

blas- = false
+
-phēmē = speech

Ever since it became fashionable to be in therapy, it has become equally fashionable to seek places to situate blame. It's gotten to the point where every unattractive aspect of ourselves can be explained as the result of someone else's influence. The most popular focus for blame is our parents. We hear, "My parents smothered me," and "My parents neglected me." Both are just part and parcel of the same blame game. I do not at all mean to dismiss the devastating consequences of a difficult childhood. I have my own experience of that, but I do deliberately mean to challenge the usefulness of blame.

Blame, as an explanation, keeps us right where we are. To quote Richard Bach, "Argue for your problems, and sure enough, they're yours." Curiously, blame and blaspheme are essentially the same word. Blasphemy, originally meaning evil speech, has become associated with contempt for God. I'd say that blame has the same emotion of contempt behind it, and what does it get us? Very little. The definition of both words is *false speech*. Blame can act as false speech in the sense that it can disempower our ability to change. (Not to mention blame's paralyzing first cousin, shame.) Ask: How can I speak truly about my life today?

Infinition:
I give up the blame game and follow one of the Buddha's precepts—Right Speech. When I speak the truth about my life without blame, I am free to change and heal.

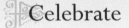

Celebrate

celeber = frequented, populous

from

caelum- = heaven

To celebrate is to honor, an old-fashioned word if ever there was one. It comes from a Latin word implying *lots of people, often in the same place*. Nowadays, celebration usually implies just that, a gathering of people in one place. Often the things we gather to honor get lost in the pageantry of the event. When was the last time you gathered to honor? What did you honor?

What if we turn our gaze to the deeper root of the word—*heaven*? Heaven is not a rented party space or a banquet hall; heaven is actually a place within each one of us. As a minister, I am called upon to celebrate all the major rites of passage in life (and some less major but no less important). I was asked once to do a wedding in a Laundromat, which was the family business. It was a beautiful wedding because the people involved were in their own heaven and honoring their own needs. When I celebrate a ceremony, whether a wedding, a divorcing, a birthing, a funeral, a clearing, a blessing of a space, or any other kind of communion, my role is to create a heavenly space where honor can happen. Ask: How can I honor myself and celebrate today?

Infinition:

I return celebration to its proper perspective in my life by honoring the things and people who are important to me no matter how big or how small.

Challenge

calumnia = a false accusation

from

calvī = to deceive

I see a Knight of Olde throwing down a gauntlet when I hear this word. I also see myself being told that whatever I want to do cannot be done, and then I see myself rising to the challenge. Challenges are often overrated in our world—at least those which come from outside us. Originally, challenge comes from the Latin, meaning *a false accusation*. Do those challenges which arise from outside us hold accusation? Sometimes. Are they false? They can be. Note that the deeper etymology for challenge is *deceit*.

Interestingly, the people who love us best in the world can challenge us into our own greatness. They see our unconscious edges and the places where we need to grow sometimes more clearly than we do ourselves. Drs. Judith Sherven and James Sniechowski, authors of *Opening to Love 365 Days a Year*, call this being "loved into greatness." When loved ones challenge us, they activate the deepest challenges that actually come from within us; our own Divine Spark calls forth the need for challenges which ultimately cause us to change and thereby grow.

When challenges come from others, a sometimes dangerous energy of competition arises and we meet the expectations of others rather than hearing the honest double dare of our own inner truth. Ask: How can I defuse the self-deceiving expectations of others and meet my own challenges today?

Infinition:
When I hear someone deceiving me with their own daring, I stop and listen within me. My own challenges are plenty for me and as I meet them, I am gracefully changed.

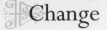Change

cambire = to exchange, or barter

We deal with change all the time, often without even noticing it. When I order in dinner from a local restaurant and I tip the delivery person, I often say simply, "Keep the change." What am I really giving here? When I say it unconsciously, I mean, "The balance of the money is yours to keep." When I say it with intention, I'm saying a blessing as well: "May your life change as you wish it to change." This, for a few coins! We even call them "small change." Sometimes I wonder if there even is such a thing as small change.

When clients come to me wanting a quick fix to change their lives, I tell them that human change isn't like turning a rowboat midstream which, if you've ever done it, you know is simple—put one oar in the water and pull. Instead, most deep change is like turning the *Queen Elizabeth II*. Stately, slow, majestic, and by God, once the captain has made that 180-degree turn, the ocean liner is turned for keeps.

The next time you handle small change, remember that you're the captain, and realize that real change is really *barter*. You *exchange* the small changes for the big change you're seeking. Ask: How can I exchange small changes for the large ones I want in my life today?

Infinition:
Change comes easily to me and I adapt well to all kinds of change. Small changes lead to the large ones I'm choosing for my life.

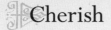Cherish

cārus = **charity**

This archaic word comes via the French word *cher*, which means *dear*. Its later root is Latin for *charity*. This is not the same kind of charity as philanthropy, although it could be. Literally, it means caring. People familiar with the older translation of the King James Version of St. Paul's epistles in the Christian Scriptures will recognize this word as part of the well-known 2nd Corinthians 13, often read at weddings, "Faith, hope, charity, these three, and the greatest of these is charity."

It's perfect that this word has come to be associated with giving, for in truth, it is natural to want to give what is dear to us, and to want to give to those who are dear to us. It's no mistake that the traditional wedding vows include cherish. Caring or charity in relating is learning how to give love the way the beloved needs caring to be. Ask: How can I charitably give care today?

Infinition:
Right now I know what is truly dear to me, and I no longer hesitate to show how I feel. I give bountifully both what is dear to me, and to those who are dear to me.

Choice

gustus = taste

Choice is the principal activity of humankind. In fact, the one gift God gave each of us is what Madeleine L'Engle calls "the terrible gift of free will." Having a free will, we are all not only entitled, but mandated (consider: commandment!) to make choices. Are you ever afraid to make a choice? A lot of us are. A large part of our fear is that it's actually possible to make a "wrong" choice, so what happens is that people simply don't choose—which is, of course, a choice in itself!

Look at the Latin etymology of the word. We choose, really, according to our *taste*, quite literally, our *gusto*. At any given time, your taste can be for one thing, so you make that choice, or at another time, another thing, so you make that choice. The simple truth about choices is that they all have consequences—they come, literally, with sequence, which is what consequence means. When you're choosing from a Chinese food menu, it doesn't seem so important whether you choose vegetables or chicken. Truly, when you choose from the menu of life, it's the same thing. Make a choice. Take that job. Ask him to marry you. Go to the gym, or not. There will always be consequences to your tastes (and choices) of the moment. If you don't like the consequences, dear one, make another choice with a light heart. Ask: How can I choose according to my own taste today?

Infinition:
I thank God for the wonderful gift of free will. I use it every single day, and the more I use it, the freer I am from the fear of choosing.

Communicate

commūn- = common (to many)
+
-facare = to make

Everyone knows that communication is the key to successful relationships. Go to any bookstore and you'll learn how Martians and Venusians can learn to speak to one another. Why, if we know that this ability is key, don't we take the time to learn how to do it? Communicate comes from the root word *common* and implies *to many*.

If I say the word *spoon* in a roomful of people, each person could easily call to mind a picture of a spoon. Will it be a sterling silver teaspoon or a wooden spoon, solid or with slats, for sherbet or grapefruit? I want to refer you back to the word *assume* because it sheds light on what is so difficult about communicating. When I say spoon, a pretty neutral word, I tend to assume that you know what kind I mean, but what if I assume that you don't? Likely there will be more words of explanation, even simple ones, and that eventually we'll both get to the same kind of spoon.

Let's up the stakes, shall we? Try it with the word *love*. You may have to explain for a long, long time but once it's common knowledge to those you love, it will mean the world to them. Ask: How can I have a common interaction today?

Infinition:
I know my communication skills can always be improved. I choose to use simple words, and explain myself whenever I must, with patience and compassion.

27

Communion

com- = together
+
-mūnis = obliging

Communion is what we are all actually seeking in our relationships. As much as we may value our individuality, we also seek a common union with the people in the world around us. Individuation and bonding are primary needs for human beings. The Latin etymology of this word is *obliging together*. What being together means is that we are obligated one to the other. When we are with others, we are obliged simply to recognize our common union.

You have, of course, heard it said that we are all connected. Buddhist monk Thich Nhat Hanh calls it "interbeing." I believe we are all in communion all the time based on, if nothing else, our breathing. How do you know that the air I exhale isn't your next inhalation? And whilst I know this isn't scientifically literal, it is a clear metaphor. Acceptance of our ultimate common union releases all fear of obligation one to another. Ask: How can I fulfill my obligation when I am with others today?

Infinition:
I enter into conscious communion now. Any sense of burden about obligation is lifted. I am joyfully together with everyone I encounter today.

Companion

com- = **together/with**

+

-pānis = **bread**

This is one of my favorite words because it sounds to me like what it promises. I have heard it said that romance is a bonus and that companionship is what we all need. Anyone who is blessed to share the life of a pet knows how wonderful "just companionship" can be! The word itself means *to share bread together*, and if you've ever eaten freshly baked bread you know that it even tastes like togetherness—warm, fresh, full.

Many everyday activities are opportunities to share companionship if we'll let them be. A walk at sunset, a drive in the car, reading aloud. I have a friend with whom I share a morning devotional daily and I know we both really look forward to those few moments of quiet bonding together. Sustenance is one of the basic needs of humanity and one of the best ways to bond with others is over a meal. We do it all the time, although I wonder if we do it consciously.

Breaking bread, in some circles, is a sacrament, and if we approach each morsel as holy we are bound to find ourselves with life-time companions—even when we are companions to ourselves. Ask: How can I share my bread together with others today?

Infinition:

My companions sustain me on my journey through life because they share their bread with me. I too share mine.

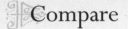

Compare

com- = **with**
+
-pare = **equality**

Comparison is one of the most dangerous traps in the spiritual life, and unfortunately, it is an intrinsic part of what we learn in school as children. By way of example, we are taught both to measure and compare ourselves to others based on our grades. Comparison leads to competition, and this NEVER WORKS in the spiritual life. There is no competition in spiritual realization; your path is uniquely your own.

Ironically, the word itself is from Latin and it means *with equality*, or on a par with. However, this is not, for the most part, how we use comparison in our world. A judgment of equality is the exception rather than the rule. Instead, we misuse it as a weapon to deem ourselves lacking in relation to others, and what a silly habit! It was that obscure philosopher Fortescue who wrote, "Comparisons are odious."

I spend an hour in meditation nearly every day. I've been meditating for more than twenty years! When someone comes to me wanting to learn to meditate, I suggest they sit for five minutes. Why should someone even be able to start at an hour? This is what we do to ourselves when we compare, on the one hand, or, if we suffer low self-esteem, we do the reverse and puff ourselves up at the expense of others. Neither is necessary or attractive. Ask: How can I see everyone on an equal par with me today?

Infinition:
I gladly give up comparing for equal status in every area of my life. My path is my own and I walk it in exactly the right way all the time.

Compromise

com- = together
+
-prōmittere = to promise

and

prō- = forth
+
-mittere = to send

In all kinds of relationships, compromise is recommended as the best solution for disagreement, and I'm sure it works for a lot of people. However, I never recommend it. In fact, I'd rather see people go their separate ways than compromise the needs of their souls. A couple came to me because they were fighting constantly. She wanted to change her career path and go to medical school; he didn't want her to do either. They worked with me for a few months and no solution was ever reached. Neither was willing *to promise together,* even though that's what they agreed on the day they got married.

The deeper Latin roots of promise mean *to send forth.* I think real compromises also mean that you are able to send yourselves forth on an entirely new path together—a bigger and better path than you've dreamed before. This means giving up needing to be right and instead choosing to be fully expressive, and to look for ways for everyone's soul needs to be met. Ask: How can I promise together with others today, so that everyone is sent forth gladly?

Infinition:

Compromise isn't about winning; it's about new and exciting paths and discoveries. I send forth my best self into all my interactions and we all send each other forth into the magic of fully expressive lives.

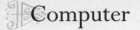Computer

com- = together
+
-*putare* = to reckon, to count

The original meaning of computer was a person who counts. It's ironic in the face of the iconography of computers—they represent the impersonal in our world. In a lovely twist, the word itself means *to reckon together*, and isn't that what we do in chat rooms? Or surfing for information? I am part of an international prayer team that is intimately connected via computer. It lets me pray with people in Africa, England, Hawaii, China. When I had surgery recently, the prayers I received were immensely helpful. There can be deep connection and value through electronic community.

I see computers as an objectification of the structure of human consciousness. The hard drive is our subconscious minds, the monitor is our conscious minds, and the keyboard is our wills. Let's go back to the original definition: imagine a person who counts, "One, two, three. . . ." And now read the words again: a person who counts. Doesn't every person count? Of course. Ask: How can I treat everyone I meet as though they count today?

Infinition:
I recognize the preciousness of each one of us on earth today. We all count, separately and together, and my behavior reflects this truth.

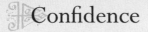Confidence

com- = **with**
+
-fidere = **trust**

Confidence is that elusive quality we all recognize in others, often seek for ourselves, and deeply wonder how to acquire. Confidence has a mystique around it. We can even smell it, and certainly we can sense when someone doesn't have it. Confidence is actually a mode of behavior. The word itself is a clue to the process of creating self-confidence. It requires that we behave *with trust*. Trust in what? Actually, the better question is: trust in whom? The answer is so obvious that it can "whiff" us.

The rabbis of old tell the story that each person carries a divine spark, an ember of G-d, within us. If we base our behavioral choices on the notion that we act with trust in the Divine Spark within us, we create self-confidence. It has been said that "God don't make junk." If Divinity created all that is, this has to include you, too. All that's required for confidence is trust in your Divine Spark. Ask: How can I act with trust in my own Divinity today?

Infinition:

Truly, a Divine Spark animates my very being. Starting right now, I take all my cues for behavior from that Spark, and I act with trust in myself.

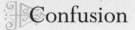Confusion

com- = **together**
+
-fundere = **to pour**

The etymology of confusion reveals the result of mixing together things which don't belong together. Usually, we think that understanding is the solution to confusion. The intellectual idea is that if you can understand something, it won't be confusing anymore. This isn't necessarily so. Werner Erhardt, the illustrious founder of the even more illustrious EST, used to say, "Understanding is the booby prize." Just because we understand doesn't mean we're empowered to go forward.

Sometimes confusion can be a way of hanging out in *I don't know*, which is really code for, *I do know, but I don't want to know* (*that I know what I know*). It can be a very clever responsibility-evasion technique! The next time you think you're confused, stop a minute and separate the things you are putting together in your thoughts. When you *pour things together*—like oil and water—that don't go together, how are you clouding the issue for yourself? What would you know if you did know? Ask: How am I pouring things together that don't go together today?

Infinition:
Because of the Divine Spark within me, I give up confusion forever. I do know what I need to know. I give myself permission to know, and to act on that knowing now.

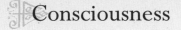Consciousness

com- = with
+
-scius = knowing

Consciousness is the part of us that is awake. When we are conscious of something, we know just what it is, and *we know* that we know. Just as there are different degrees of awakeness, there are different degrees of consciousness. To be truly conscious, which I believe is the spiritual goal to be sought above all others, we must consider its best antonym: innocence. To be innocent is to be completely unknowing.

I was hired once to give a series of seminars on a healthy work ethic for the Gila River Indian Nation. One of my students was angry that a white woman was the teacher, and he asked me, quite hostilely, if I had ever been marginalized or if I even knew what that meant. Here's what I said to him. "Yes, I know what it is to be marginalized. I am female clergy after all, but am I a Gila River Indian, and do I know what it is to be marginalized for that? No, I'm not, and, no, I don't. In my commitment to be in service here, I could make mistakes that might offend you. Here is what I propose: Instead of assuming that I'm marginalizing you, will you please assume I'm innocent, and educate me?"

In that case, I allowed myself to be fully conscious of what I might not know—sometimes equally as valuable as knowing what I do know. I asked my new friend to help me stay awake. To be fully conscious is to be fully awake to all that I do know and to all of my innocence as well. Ask: How am I using my knowing today?

Infinition:
I am grateful to know what I know. I expand my consciousness with deliberate intent to know, and to know that I know even more.

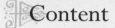Content

com- = together
+
-tenere = to hold

In the Christian Scriptures, St. Paul wrote to the people at Philippi, "I have learned, in whatsoever state I am, therewith to be content." Over the years I've gotten distracted by desires for happiness and joy, and now, I'm back to wondering about contentment. Since I was a child, I have wondered whether I would ever be content with myself, my life, what I have, who I am, why I'm here—the basic, huge questions we all have about reality. At this point, I have contentment, although I do welcome growth and change. The word itself means *to hold together.*

Here's how contentment works in a life: first, look at the CONtent—namely, what your life holds for you. Contentment comes from the stuff and substance of your life. Your spiritual practice. Your relationships. Your work. Your passion. Your play. If the content is what you've chosen, then it's easy to be content with everything. Ask: How can I change the content of my life today?

Infinition:
Contentment is mine because I love the content of my life. If I don't love the content, I change it, and I bask in contentment.

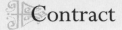Contract

com- = together
+
***-trahere* = to draw**

Every day on earth we deal with the principle of polarity. Up, down. Left, right. Over, under. Matter asks for polarity. A contract *draws together* the intentions of two or more people. I've heard attorneys refer to "reducing" a contract to writing. Interesting, isn't it, that this makes the word conTRACT (not CONtract) make sense? Maybe they're the same! With all of the polarities in life, it's hard to remember that life, like the ocean tides, ebbs, and flows. Sometimes when we experience contraction, it comes from a place of fear.

Anne Morrow Lindbergh wrote of this in her *Gift from the Sea*. "We have so little faith in the ebb and flow of life, of love, of relationships. We leap to the flow of the tide, and resist in terror at its ebb." It's important to remember that we, too, need to ebb just as much as we need to flow. Look at the Latin etymology of contract. It means *a drawing together*. Next time you need to conTRACT, instead of coming from fear, come from knowing that you are drawing yourself together, and that flow always follows ebb. Drawing up a clear and deliberate CONtract with yourself about your need to ebb will truly give you the courage you need to flow into the next phase of your life. Ask: How can I allow myself to contract when I need to and trust that I'll expand when that need arises today?

Infinition:
I understand the flow of life and where I fit into it at all times. Instead of being afraid when I need to contract, I choose to trust and I expand in that choice.

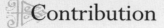Contribution

com- = together
+
-*tribuere* = to bestow; also, of the tribe

Over the years, I've done spiritual counseling with thousands of people. This word has arisen again and again as something each of their hearts desired. They would say, "I want to make a contribution to the world." It's natural that we want this. I always ask them what that means to them. It's different for each one of us. I've heard answers as diverse as, "I want to create a happy family," to "I want to win the Nobel Peace Prize."

To contribute means, from the Latin, *to bestow together*, and further, *of the tribe*. These parallel each other. First, let's take as a working premise that each of us does have a contribution to make to the world. Second, that each contribution is a bestowal, a gift, and third, that it comes from the place inside us where we know we belong, our tribe. The person who creates wonderful radio shows probably wouldn't be happy as the Secretary of Transportation. That's the point: Your contribution is yours alone to make. Ask: How can I bestow my gifts today?

Infinition:

I know I belong here and that I have a contribution to make. I applaud the contributions of others and I make the one that only I can make.

Control

contra- = against
+
-rotula = a wheel

Ever met a control freak? Ever been one? (If not, check for your halo because it's certain you're a saint.) I know it's not traditional etymology, but whenever I feel like I'm being a control freak, I see this word as "with a troll." It can feel like a troll is in charge when I'm coming from the fear that causes the kind of need to control that a control freak has. It took me years to get a handle on my emotions, and I ran my life as though I were their victim. Through meditation, I tamed the troll and began to be able to make choices about my emotions, including how to express them.

The word control means *against a wheel*, in the sense that car brakes are "against" tires. The tires don't take the brakes personally, and brakes do allow one to stop when necessary. The thing about control is that we are never correct in controlling others or even situations; we are only correct in controlling ourselves. In fact, since we can only control ourselves, it's far better to set our sights on that than to set up failure by trying to control others. When you give up controlling others, life becomes a lot more peaceful. Ask: How can I control only myself today?

Infinition:
I have been given dominion over myself at all times, in all circumstances, and in all places. I accept that I am in control of me, and me alone. Otherwise, I let go and let God work out the details.

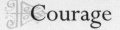

Courage

cor = **heart**

In *The Wizard of Oz*, the Cowardly Lion goes off to see the Wizard in hopes of getting "the noive"; the Tin Man, a heart; and the Scarecrow, a brain. Interesting, isn't it, that the noive is right up there with the two most important organs in the body? What nerve is it? It's a physiological one—the vagus nerve—and it's directly linked to the heart. In Oz, the noive is understood to be courage. The Lion has the heart, but he needs the *oomph* to act on it.

The word courage comes to us via the Old French *coeur* which means, literally, *heart*. How do these holy three—courage, heart and brain—fit together? In his definition of courage, that other dictionary author Dr. Webster tells us that mind, heart, spirit are synonyms for courage. Wondrous that L. Frank Baum does the same: Brain, Heart, Nerve.

What courage really represents is Spirit, the spirit of following our own inner wisdom. The brain chooses, based on the heart's whispers, and courage allows us to act. Ask: How can I have the courage to follow my heart and my brain today?

Infinition:
I meet life with mind, heart, and courage in all circumstances. If I feel my heart and spirit disconnect, I wait till I can act with courage.

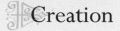

Creation

creare = **to bring forth**

One of the New Age mantras is that we create our own reality. This is true . . . except . . . that when there is even one other person involved in what we're creating, we have to remember that we are co-creating. This means that the simple *bringing forth* that we can do on our own, like making a tuna fish sandwich, is suddenly exponentially complicated.

Let's look at this Latin etymology on a bigger scale. You know that in order to create anything, you have to use your free will and make a choice, so now you've decided: you're choosing to create a Cadillac and a soul mate. Okay. Manifesting the Cadillac is much easier than manifesting the soul mate. For the Caddy, it's you, your checkbook, the local Cadillac dealership, and the machine. All things being provided for, you go, write the check, and drive off toward home in your new, elegant wheels. The soul mate is a different story because there's another soul involved. How do you know your soul mate isn't healing from a divorce? Or maybe she needs to care for aging parents first? Or maybe he is switching careers and needs time to get settled? You don't. So you do the same thing you would do for a Cadillac—you choose, and then you wait till it brings itself forth.

This is what co-bringing forth is about: specify and surrender, and let the results show up in their own time, all the while remembering that God is co-creating right along with you. Ask: How can I bring forth my best today?

Infinition:
When I can create on my own, I do it joyfully. When I am co-creating, I am patience itself as I await what I am bringing forth in love.

Crisis

krīnein = to separate

This word comes to us from medical Latin and refers to the defining moment in a disease process, in the sense that a fever breaking is a crisis point. You might have heard it said in metaphysical circles, "He's in a healing crisis." Sometimes this can feel like an oxymoronic euphemism, and upon occasion can fall into the category of what I call "metaphysical malpractice." However, there are often organic crises in healing, and the Greek etymology explains their purpose.

A crisis is really a stopping point—full stop, do not pass Go, do not collect $200, a stop-and-pay-attention place. Its purpose is *to separate* life into two sections: life before the crisis, and life after it. If we'll look deeply into ourselves, we can almost always find a corollary psychospiritual aspect to physical disease. This is the gift of crisis. It separates us from our everyday lives, and sounds a wake-up call. Ask: How can I be awake without the need of a crisis today?

Infinition:
Crisis is sometimes necessary, and right now I determine to give up "doing drama" over crisis. Instead, I choose to meet and respond to the crises in my life with deep looking, listening, and learning. I am open to the gift of crisis.

Death

deth = death

from

datum = given

Here's a subject to be avoided! Psychologists say that death is the ultimate fear for most people, and yet we experience death daily in one way or another. The sun dies each night and is reborn in the morning. Our cells die daily. I'm sure you've heard that every seven years every single cell in our bodies dies and is replaced. Why are we so afraid of death? I believe it really depends on what you believe about it. If you think you're going to heaven, you'll experience heaven when you die. If you think you're going to spend a lot of time with the worms, then you'll meet worms. And every other thought you have in between.

As far as I know, every single one of us will die, and the deeper Latin etymology tells us why. Death is *a given*. Part of the deal here. The end of the contract. We know we will die and few of us know when. So? Since it's a given, what do you say we get on with the business of living and let death meet us when it's time? Ask: How can I deal with the given of death today in a life-giving way?

Infinition:

I face my fear of death today, and it's not so bad. Death is an inevitable part of life. Once my fear is gone, I see death as a valuable part of my life.

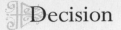Decision

de- = from
+
-caedēre = to cut away

    The process of decision-making is fraught with anguish for some of us. Deciding is similar to choosing, yet with an important difference. Choosing works with things both tangible and intangible. Deciding almost always has an air of finality to it. This job or that job? This girlfriend? This fiancé? This apartment? That house? This Jaguar or that Jeep? Choosing seems to imply that we still have options; deciding implies that we leave certain options behind forever. Of course, the etymology of the word explains the reason.

    Like incision, which means to cut into, decision means *to cut away from*. I find that when I make a decision and am unhappy with it, changing it usually means having to do what I call "emotional K.P." Kitchen Police, a term from the military, is the least appealing kind of duty to draw. Yet it's not that bad. So I have to do cleanup. I think of the miles of litter sponsors on America's highway system. There's a section in Queens proudly bearing a sign with the name Bette Midler. She picks up the trash in the area. If Bette gets to do the garbage brigade, why not me? Or you? Ask: How can I cut away the discomfort around deciding today?

Infinition:

    Decisions are clear to me when I approach them from the clear place inside me—my Divine Spark. Holy scissors make deciding easy.

Definite

de- = from

+

-fīnis = a boundary

The idea that we all should have boundaries is one of the major teachings of all the Twelve-Step programs. Basically, the message is that it is our personal responsibility to choose what we accept into our experience and what we reject as unacceptable. Would that boundaries were as black and white as that! Boundaries are definite, without question, but only in the moment because some boundaries can change. Definite, by definition, means coming *from a boundary* or a limit. When my kitty, Charles, yowls too much, I tell him, "That's enough," and he has come to understand exactly what I mean.

The secret to managing boundaries and being definite is to stay flexible. Boundaries shift depending upon circumstances. I vowed years ago to keep to myself on the city streets. The other day I saw a young boy teasing a schoolgirl. It was clear to me that they knew each other and were friends, but that he was going beyond the pale. I intervened for her, and asked the boy quite forcibly, "What part of *No* do you not understand?" He backed off and apologized to both of us, and I was able to explain somewhat more calmly that when anyone says *No*, it's best to take it to heart. So much for keeping to myself. Yet another boundary made boundless. Ask: How can I be definite for today and change it when required?

Infinition:

I am aware of my boundaries and I speak my truth about them when necessary. Even better, when necessary, I bound right past my old boundaries and create new ones.

Deliver

de- = **from**
+
-līberare = **to set free**

It never occurred to me until I looked up the etymology of deliver that when a messenger delivers an envelope to me, she is actually setting the envelope free, but that's exactly what happens! If we look at everyday deliveries in this way, there's a lot more liberating going on around us than we'd thought. The Latin roots of deliver mean *from setting free*. Freedom is a great concern in the West, and despite that we take our freedoms for granted a lot of the time.

Right now, let's focus our concern for freedom where we truly live: our bodies. The liver is the organ notorious for processing any toxins we take in, including our feelings, especially anger and primitive emotions, according to Religious Science minister, Louise Hay. When we de-liver, we set ourselves free from toxins and anger. That makes it more personal! Anger is just energy. Why keep it in our bodies? There are appropriate ways to free ourselves from anger. Liberation awaits! Ask: How can I de-liver myself into peace today?

Infinition:
I deliver myself into a nontoxic life. If de-liverance is necessary, so be it.

Denial

de- = **away**

+

-negare = **to refuse**

Gleaned from the lexicon of psychological jargon, the word denial is by now a well-established word in pop culture. Imagine my surprise when I was researching it and read, "See renegade." Renegade? What happens when we *refuse away* parts of our knowing into the unconscious mind is that they become renegade in our psyches. Denial, as they say, ain't a river in Egypt. It is mystically, though. If you'll look up the deeper meaning of Egypt in a mystical bible dictionary (the best one is *The Metaphysical Bible Dictionary* by Charles Fillmore), it represents the unconscious aspect of mind. Ironically (or not), denial, in the Psych 101 sense, is all about the unconscious aspect of Self. Of course.

For years I struggled with my body, eating, dieting, food, exercise until one day I threw my scale out an eleventh-story window (into an alley!) and decided to get out of denial that I had a problem with my body image and eating. It took me twenty-six years. In those years, talk about renegade thoughts and ideas! I lied to myself, others, family, friends. I denied the truth about the problem, and jeepers, what trouble I caused myself. When I discovered that I was swimming in that river in Egypt, I climbed out, dried off, and accepted the dare of my own Spirit to heal. Ask: How can I harness my refusal away of truth for healing today?

Infinition:

Denial has served its purpose in my life, and now I climb out of that river of refusal and into the acceptance of my fullest truth. Whatever needs healing draws its own resources to me now, and I rejoice to be in total acceptance of what is.

Desire

dē- = **from**
+
-sīderes = **heavenly body**

I was married to an artist for some years, and I know, as surely as I'm sitting at a computer right now, that he paints because he cannot NOT paint. I know that Mozart felt the same way about writing music. I know that when I love deeply, I feel the desire to make love because I cannot not make love with my beloved. This sort of desire is sometimes called "God-given." God does give us our true heart desires. Not in the sense of granting them like a genie. God-given desires arise in our hearts *so that* we will seek them.

The word itself shows us this ineffable truth: desire means *from the heavenly body*. Taking the whole of Divinity metaphorically as a body, it must be so that the Divine Body is heavenly. The natural activity of all bodies is desire. It is our ordained mission to seek and find the heavenly fulfillment of our desires. Ask: How can I let my heart desires rise into my knowing today?

Infinition:
My true desires are given to me by God and as such they always deserve fulfillment. I allow myself to feel desire today, and I love how alive it makes me feel.

Despair

de- = reversal
+
-spei = of hope

Despair lies at the outer reaches of the human emotional spectrum. It's a place in our psyches most of us would like to be able to avoid, although sometimes I wonder at the wisdom of avoiding it. The more we limit what we are willing to feel, the fewer feelings we have until it is possible to become an emotional Johnny One Note. At the other end of the spectrum, I would place bliss. Without the willingness to experience despair, bliss becomes unavailable to us as well. The etymology of the word despair reveals that they are inextricably linked.

Despair means *a reversal of hope*. Alexander Pope wrote, "Hope springs eternal in the human breast." I believe it does even when hope appears entirely absent. We are reminded all the time about the reliability of God. The sun comes up. The tides ebb and flow. Acorns grow oak trees and not weeping willows. There is an order to this universe, and we are a part of it. That's what gives us hope, so when you find yourself at the hopeless and despairing end of the emotional rainbow, turn yourself in the direction of bliss. The sun will come up tomorrow, just as Little Orphan Annie always promised. Ask: How can I reverse hopelessness for myself or someone else today?

Infinition:

I am committed to a full experience of life here on earth. Despair comes, bliss comes, and I am unattached to either. Instead, I choose to allow all of my feelings space to breathe.

Dictionary

dictio = a saying

from

dīcere = to speak

It seems only right for *God's Dictionary* to include a definition of what a dictionary actually is. Originally, dictionaries were about diction. In other words, how to say what we say. The Latin roots mean *to speak,* not to define. When something is defined, it is in fact limited, made less broad.

Were God to speak about *God's Dictionary*, here's what I think we'd hear: "A dictionary is a resource for choosing words which express who you really choose to be. Spend some time with your dictionary looking up the ordinary words you use every day and discover what you're really saying about yourself. If you like them and what speaking those words has made of your life, great. If not, keep looking; there are millions of other words to choose from. Your words create your life. People ask all the time for an instruction book for life. There's probably a dictionary gathering dust on your shelf right now. Take it down, blow off the dust, and treat yourself to a new word each day." Ask: How can I speak the life I choose into being today?

Infinition:
I have a resource for words at my fingertips. All dictionaries hold clues to the real meanings of the words I speak. Now, I speak truly of my life choices.

Disappointment

dis- = not
+
-appoint = chosen

As I wrote in the Introduction, this is the word that tipped me into the power of words to heal. My mother's worst condemnation was, "I'm so disappointed in you." It meant we children hadn't behaved in a way of which she approved. The legacy of this childhood refrain for me was the experience of constant disappointment as an adult. Nothing ever met my unconscious expectations. Ever. Look at the word. When one is appointed to a position, for example, one is chosen. *Ergo*, when one is *dis*appointed, one is *not chosen*. Ouch!

Let's go deeper. Disappointment arises from a French phrase *à point*, literally, to a point. It usually happens when we've decided on the point or outcome we want from a situation, and it hasn't turned out the way we thought we wanted it to turn out. Double ouch! Anyone recognize attachment here? Often the feeling of disappointment is really inviting us to make a bigger (read: better for you) choice. Ask: How can I choose bigger today?

Infinition:

If ever I am disappointed, I choose again trusting that God is guiding me to better choices than the one I originally thought I wanted.

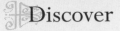Discover

dis- = not
+
-operire = to hide

Just after I got my driver's license, I took my baby brother John, then six, to an art museum for the afternoon. We were wandering at that museum pace people use when we came upon a Jackson Pollock string painting. John looked at it, and then up at me, and said, "That's a barn, and that's a cow." I remember standing very still after his statement. If you'll picture a Jackson Pollock string painting in your mind's eye, you will know that he didn't paint barns or cows, but that was what John saw.

I discovered something important that day, or rather, two somethings were not hidden from me any longer. First, that whatever we bring to anything is what we discover in it. Second, that whatever is hidden is there for discovery if we'll allow ourselves to see it. Anything in this universe is available for our discovery if we choose *not to hide* from it. This includes all that we have to learn about ourselves. There is nothing any of us can discover that will make us less lovable to God. Ask: How can my life be about not hiding today?

Infinition:
Life is a great adventure of discovery for me. If I was hiding, I'm not hiding anymore. I'm an explorer of consciousness and what I discover is delicious.

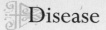Disease

dis- = not
+
-esse = to be

There is, in spiritual circles, a definition of disease that qualifies as metaphysical malpractice if you ask me. This is: "not at ease." My initial reaction to this thinking is just to laugh because some people are actually quite fond of their illnesses, supremely *at ease* with them in fact. Ironically (or not), the world itself tells us the truth about itself. It means, literally, *not to be*. DO YOU KNOW WHAT THAT MEANS? I just want to stand up and scream! (I'll calm down in a moment but . . . just for the record why don't we calm up?) What it means is that disease is not meant to be.

All of the New Age or Bronze Age or whatever Age belief systems that try to tell us that disease is absolutely a part of us—or absolutely not a part of us for that matter (Have you ever heard someone refer to a part of their own body as "the back" or "the leg"? I always want to say, "What leg? The one you keep in the hall closet? It's YOUR leg!")—are all wrong. Disease is not meant to be, it's not ordained, not in the natural order of things, and it sure ain't anybody's fault. Disease is a reality of the facts of life but it is not to be the Truth of life, and should be treated as such, not as the center or the heart of our lives. Ask: How can I allow disease not to be the center of my being today?

Infinition:
I use my Spirit to put disease in its proper place, and in doing so I allow myself and others to be healed.

Distrust

dis- = not
+
-trust = firm

Over the years, so many people have come to me with "trust issues" in their lives and we would work and work at finding their causes. Certain things in our lives we just trust. When I get on the M104 bus going down Broadway, I don't ask the driver what route she'll be driving. I know the route, and if she plans to deviate from it, she'll tell me. If we really had trust issues, we'd have to check everything. Can you imagine? Is there really toothpaste in that tube? What's the fertilizer that farmer used on the carrots in my fridge? You take my meaning.

Distrust is a habit, the habit of suspicion, and it has absolutely nothing to do with anything outside us, nothing at all. It's something we learn, and we learn it through experience. We internalize what for us is *not firm*, not stable, not true. Those of us who have had the dubious opportunity to heal abuse of any kind know how we learned distrust, but it's really not important how we learned to distrust. What is important is what we do with the habit now. Somewhere deep inside our Spirits we know that trust is just as viable and ultimately the easier choice than distrust, no matter what happened in the past. Ask: How can I deal kindly with what's not firm in me today?

Infinition:
I choose to trust the goodness of the universe from now on. No matter what conclusions I've drawn based on the past, I choose to trust again and again. It's such a relief.

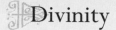# Divinity

deiwos = shining

God. Goddess. Buddha. Lao-tse. Confucius. Kwan Yin. Kali.
Aphrodite. Zeus. The Green Man. Jesus. Mary. The Force. Sheila Na
Gig. Infinite Intelligence. Ganesh. Saraswati. I could go on, and I
needn't. I truly believe that Divinity by any other name would smell
as sweet. The point isn't *what* you call It, the point is *that* you call It.
The image I use for Divinity is the largest, most faceted diamond in
the universe. In fact, It is the universe. If you've ever seen an uncut
diamond, you know that the facets are what make diamonds so appealing. The facets catch and reflect the light.

The Indo-European root of Divinity means *shining*, which goes
perfectly with my diamond metaphor. If the universe is a diamond,
then everything in the universe is a part of the diamond. Each part is
a facet, and each is designed to catch and reflect the light. We've all
seen pictures of Mother Teresa, so we know what the shining looks
like when a facet is fully available to the Original Shining, otherwise
known as _____. Fill in whatever name(s) you choose today and
change them whenever you so choose. And remember, She doesn't
care what you call Her, He cares that you call Him. Ask: How can I
let the shining through my facet of the diamond today?

Infinition:
My name for Divinity may change from day to day and this fact
notwithstanding I let my light shine.

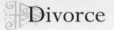Divorce

di- = not
+
-versus = right

More than half the marriages in the United States end in divorce. I've had couples come to me asking that I officiate their weddings, who have literally said, "Well, if it doesn't work, we can always get divorced." I send them packing. But what about the couple who have "done it all right"? They got married in good faith, certain it would work. They've worked at their relationship. They've gotten help when they needed it, and still it isn't working. This word is for them.

Divorce means *not right*, and whilst the marriage fundamentalists in the world will see this definition as a judgment on the act of divorce itself, I see it as a description of the circumstances that justify the act. Divorce is the right decision when you've done all you can and things are not right, and aren't going to get right in the reasonable future. The truth is, souls are a mystery. The primary mandate for each of us is to grow. Sometimes we can grow through staying the course in our relationships, no question. Other times, the path of growth is to be found in straying from the course of our relationships.

When a relationship of any kind in your life isn't right, at some level you know it. You might try a temporary divorce and see if it is right. Ask: How can I acknowledge what's not right in my life today?

Infinition:
Divorce may feel like the option of failure. When there is anything not right in any area of my life, within myself or with others, I work at it and then I trust enough to let go so we can all grow.

Doubt

from
duo = two

Doubt plagues all of us. Often it's part of the decision-making process, and even part of choosing. I think doubt teaches us about our true natures. I applied to undergraduate school on the early-decision program. It meant that I could apply to only one school, and that I'd know if I got in by Thanksgiving instead of waiting for the usual springtime reply. Between the time of the application and my receipt of the answer, I swung between the extremes of supreme confidence and deep doubt in myself.

Here is the message: when you are in doubt, you are approaching a matter from the level of your Soul, and not from the level of your Spirit. Soul is about multiplicity and Spirit is about Unity. You will receive undivided, clear messages from your Spirit, and sometimes divided, doubtful ones from your Soul. The word is based on *two*. Two—or sometimes, if you're a Libra like me— seven-mindedness. When in doubt, wait.

In Jewish spiritual practice, the strongest statement of faith is the *Shema* which is: "Hear, O Israel, the Lord Our God is One." You can find it in the Book of Deuteronomy 6:4, in the Hebrew Bible. Listen deeply to your Spirit. It is the Spark of God within you. It has one voice, one message, one idea—that you grow in love. Ask: How can I be still and use my doubts to help me get the one clear message today?

Infinition:
Doubt is my friend. It gifts me with the chance to get clearer and clearer about who I am and who I'm meant to be, fully in my Spirit, with myself and others.

Dysfunctional

dys- = not
+
-functio = perform

I love what graphic artist Mary Englebreit suggests we do with dysfunction: Let's put the fun back in dysFUNctional. Is anyone else tired of hearing about dysfunctional families? Workplaces? Relationships? With all due respect, and I happen to be intimate with growing up in a dysfunctional, alcoholic family myself, I'm with Mary. We all grew up with dysfunction to one degree or another. I think dysfunction is a function of the American Dream, which arose from the aftermath of the Second World War. Like the television household of June and Ward Cleaver, everything had to look good whether it was good or not.

Wherever it came from, the real question is: What are we going to do about it now? The word tells us what to do: *not perform*. Of course, it means something which is not performing its proper purpose, but I see it another way. One of the major pieces of dysfunction is making what others are thinking about us more important than what we think of ourselves. What happens then is, we perform, and are therefore inauthentic, for the sake of image.

Dysfunction sends us a message: Don't perform (to anyone else's expectations), live your authentic life instead. When we stop the performance and begin to live our real lives, I'm pretty sure we'll find that dysfunction falls apart all by itself. Ask: How can I live authentically today?

Infinition:
I choose no longer to live based on dysfunction of any kind. In fact, I can't because I choose to be fully functional in every way. I live my true, fun life.

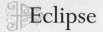Eclipse

ek- = out
+
-leipein = to leave

Ordinarily, when we think of eclipses, we think of the solar and lunar kinds; in recent years there have been many. When I look at this word though, I have a specific emotional response to it. Have you ever been in a group of people and felt eclipsed? The Greek roots will tell you what I mean: *left out*. I have felt lonelier in groups of people than I have ever felt all by myself. What is that about?

There was a man I knew in seminary, who shall remain nameless. Whenever he walked into any room where I was, I felt invisible, just like when the light of a heavenly body is obscured from my vision by another body in front of it. I can't tell you to this day why I felt this way in his presence. There was no logical reason. It's been years since I've seen him, too, so I can't tell you if I'd feel this way today, but what I can tell you is how I dealt with it.

I used classical metaphysical denial and affirmation. I denied the power I was somehow giving him by using Emilie Cady's famous statement, "There is no such personality in all the universe." Then I affirmed myself using words uttered by Eleanor Roosevelt, "No one can make me feel inferior without my consent." Ask: How can I be sure not to leave anyone out today?

Infinition:
I have no need to eclipse anyone I meet. I open my heart and include everybody, even those people I don't always like, in my heart of compassion.

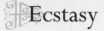Ecstasy

ec- = out of
+
-stasis = place

To be in stasis means to be in a state of inert equilibrium. This motionless equilibrium is close kin to that elusive something many of us are secretly seeking, customarily called security. Security is a much sought-after commodity—paychecks, benefits, the right caregivers, the right spouse. Together these things allegedly give us the complete sense of well-being we talk about when we mean security. In truth, none of these things can give us security although we tell ourselves they do. My friend Milt always says, "The problem with trying to find the place [of security] is that once you find it, they moved it." There is no "place" outside ourselves where we can find security. It is within us. Once we realize this, there is a whole lot more room to move. Suddenly, we can explore alternatives to the static security to which we've been taught to cling.

The alternative is *ecstasy*, which is the result of living in the Divine Flow of life. Ecstasy is a feeling we'd all like to have, and its very nature demands that we live in an undesignated, even "insecure" place. The word means *out of place*, which most of us would take to be an uncomfortable place to be. Not so. To live in Divine Flow is literally to be out of place in the world. Why? Because it cannot by its very nature be static. It is a flow. Having tried security, I find it overrated. I'd rather live my days taking the risks that arise in my life and braving the chance for ecstasy to be part of my experience. So if you want ecstasy to enter your life, let go, go with the flow and watch for miracles, synchronicities, and dreams come true. Ask: How can I get out of the place I'm always in today?

Infinition:

I'm through with playing it safe in the name of security. Starting right now, I risk so I can learn, grow, and thrive. I am ecstatic.

Ego

ego = I

Here's an old bugaboo, especially in the spiritual life. The ego has been given a bad rap as far as I'm concerned. Clients of mine have asked me for years if a desire or feeling in themselves or others is "coming from ego," and they never mean it to be a good thing. Their question comes from the Eastern spiritual traditions, which suggest that the surrender of the ego is the way to enlightenment. I have no problem with that, if that's your path, but I ask you sincerely, how can you surrender what you don't have? In order to surrender the ego, you need to have a sense of ego first.

The word itself means *I,* that sense of myself as different from you. Note that in the Hebrew Bible, God names Itself I AM—ego is the very first name of God! So what's a soul to do? Strengthen ego? Surrender ego? Another option? Yes, there is. I've said it before, and I'll say it many times again: The task here on earth is to grow. So first, we grow a sense of I, a sense of self as distinct from others. Then we use our Spirit, the I AM, to infuse the ego and surrender it to God. Think on this. If I AM is a name for God, then we must always put on the other side of those words something which is True. Do you think God tells Itself, "I am so stupid," or, "I am fat," or "I am never going to amount to anything?" Of course not.

Begin to use your ego on your spiritual path to choose the truth about who you are. Say to yourself, "I am brilliant. I am beautiful. I am glad to be exactly who I am." Then surrender to God. Ask: How can I tell myself the truth today?

Infinition:

My ego is under construction, and I AM is the builder. I let the Spirit of Truth inform every thought I think and every word that passes my lips, and I surrender effortlessly.

Emergency

ē- = out
+
-mergere = to dive

One of the many shows for which I was the production stage manager in college was *The Hobbit*. One night, in the final scene, a huge, heavy piece of scenery came down out of the flies perfectly on cue. However, when it hit the stage, the ropes stretched and it kept on coming, crashing down on the star of the show. I am a person who is excellent in an emergency. I walked out onto the stage, picked up what I later discovered was an almost five-hundred-pound set piece, rescued the Hobbit, and she finished the show. So did I. Hours later I shook with fear.

Emergency demands that we *dive out* of ourselves. I think sometimes that this is why we continually create them. They literally force us to emerge from our everyday habits of complacency. Get up, go to work, come home. These can become the same old, same old very easily. When we dive out of ourselves, we discover things we couldn't otherwise know about ourselves. Ask: How can I dive out of myself without creating an emergency today?

Infinition:
If emergencies arise in my life, I take them as opportunities to emerge out of the comfortable self I've created. I gladly leave the same old cocoon for my soaring, butterfly nature.

Enlightenment

en- = in
+
-lighten- = bright, kindle
+
-ment

Ah! The goal of all spiritual practice! But what, exactly, is enlightenment? There are all sorts of lofty, and noble, ideas about what it is floating around in the ethers. Enlightenment always seems to conjure up an exalted state of being and yet, despite its proper status as a noun, the word has the etymology of a verb! Could it be that it's an exalted state of doing? The daily task of enlightenment is to *kindle* your experience.

If you've ever built a fire in a fireplace, you know that kindling is the small pieces of wood that catch fire before the big logs catch on. What kindling does is prepare the fire, and this is the point to the process of enlightenment. The Zen tradition says, "Before enlightenment? Chop wood, carry water. After enlightenment? Chop wood, carry water."

The point is that enlightenment isn't about a destination at all. It's about *how* you live your life in every single moment, how you do what you do. Having the goal to embody the Godself fully makes daily experience brighter, and your spiritual practice is the kindling. Ask: How can I enlighten, enbrighten, and enkindle my life today?

Infinition:
I choose spiritual fire as a metaphor for my daily living. I expect my life to be bright with blessing, and if it dims, I add kindling.

Enthusiasm

en- = in possession of
+
-theós = God

Cool is in, and it has been for a long time. Cool can be a pose, a posture, a way of watching life as opposed to participating in life. I've never been cool. In fact, I've always been quite warm. I can never sit back and observe another person who needs a hug, a handkerchief, or a listening ear. In fact, I'm the first volunteer. I feel genuine enthusiasm about the nature of humankind. I believe it's because I see God in everyone and in myself.

The original meaning of this word is *in possession of God* or *possessed by a God*, in the sense of being inspired. I love the idea that I am God's possession, and the truth is that God literally inspires (read: breathes in) me. I belong to God, and some days, I even feel like a prized possession (although I suspect I am a prized possession every day whether I feel like it or not). So I never choose cool. I always choose enthusiasm. Ask: How can I let God possess me today?

Infinition:
I love the feeling of enthusiasm that rushes through me when I get to show how warm I really am. I am God's precious possession, and it inspires me to enthusiasm.

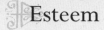
Esteem

æ- = from
+
-*stimāre* = to value

A lack of self-esteem is often named as the core of all psychological difficulty. In truth, it's a simple matter of measuring *value*. When we esteem someone else, we measure their value to us. What system of measurement do you use? There are all kinds of measuring devices. The one closest to home is your own heart. Let your value of yourself and others arise from within you.

My closest friend from college and I have been friends for more than twenty years. I know that she is a brilliant thinker and strategist, and I hold her ability in high esteem. When I am having trouble sorting out something in my life, I can count on her to straighten out my thinking every time. You might ask if I don't esteem myself enough to be able to do it myself? Sometimes, but Barbra Streisand is right: People who need people are the luckiest people in the world. I need my friend's clear mind. Part of valuing her ability is having some of it rub off on me.

The fastest way I know to self-esteem is to listen within and use your own standard for measuring value. Ask: How can I value myself and others today?

Infinition:
Self-esteem is no longer an issue for me. My value is assured in my eyes and in the eyes of God because it comes from within me. As I value myself and others, my value increases.

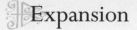Expansion

ex- = from
+
-pandere = to spread out

You have seen, I'm sure, the Taoist symbol of change called yin/yang. In the dark, contracting, yin side, there is a small dollop of light. In the light, expanding yang side, there is a small dollop of dark. What most viewers forget is that the symbol, while printed and static, actually represents motion; it's a depiction of the interplay between expansion and contraction. We in the West often favor expansion over contraction. We seem to feel that bigger is always better. Perhaps, but what if we're talking about something like poison ivy? Then I think not.

Expansion is about *spreading out* our minds, ideas, expressions, influences. The trick to living through expansion is to prepare for contraction to come soon after because, like the yin/yang, contraction is included in expansion and vice versa. When the title for this book came to me, I was in a hugely creative period of expansion. Ideas came fast and furious, and so did opportunities. I wrote the proposal and then I had to wait in a contracted time. Once the book sold, expansion followed contraction, as promised.

What happens is, when we're in expansion mode, we forget this, and then are upset at contraction. Don't worry. They follow one another as night follows day. Ask: How can I spread out today?

Infinition:
I know all about the rhythm of the universe. I both expand and contract with ease because I know they contain one another.

Explanation

ex- = **from**
+
-plānus = **level**

My son Isaac died the day he was born, and you can believe me when I tell you that I not only asked God for an explanation, I demanded one. Over and over again. It seemed to me that a child dying before its parents was definitely out of order. Now, years later, I have to wonder at myself.

Explanation means, literally, *to make plain,* but it also has a deeper meaning. The Latin etymology, *from level,* reveals that explanation is not so much about what is made clear and understandable, but what just is. We've all heard the expression *to level* the playing field. Explanations often come simply in the form of the basic ground on which we walk, the what is, if we'll look for them. And while explanations have intrinsic value, like why we mustn't rest a hand on a hot burner, they also can rob us of mystery. An explanation, which I did in fact eventually receive from God many years later, isn't always necessary or helpful.

Sometimes the path of wisdom is, as poet Rainer Maria Rilke wrote, "to live the questions." To live in and with mystery is to live without the need always to understand and thereby explanation becomes moot. Mystery is intriguing and very sweet. Ask: How can I make level the ground and make plain what it is I must know today?

Infinition:

I make peace with mystery. I understand that all things do not need to be explained nor are explainable. I am content to live the questions and wait for revelation.

Family

famel = a servant

At times this word is enough to make the strongest of us cringe. I believe that our souls choose our biological families as the perfect laboratories to test and strengthen us. It took me a long time to figure it out, but now I truly believe that some part of me agreed to my father being killed in a plane crash when I was six years old. Maybe it wasn't the optimal plan, but it definitely focused me on dealing with abandonment issues.

The original meaning of the word family is from an ancient Italian tribe whose language was Oscan, and it refers to *a servant,* or a group of household servants. Could it be that the original concept of family emerged out of a household with servants? Perhaps our fundamental role in a family, be it biological or of our own choosing, is to serve one another? I think it is. We can also trace our word *familiar* to this root.

We are familiar with those in our families, so we'll be both their servants and their masters; another way to think of this is as being both students and teachers. Often, we have to get away from our families to see what the lessons have been. Ask: How can I serve and be served by my family today?

Infinition:
Blood families are only one type. It is also my option to create a postbiological, sacred family. I choose where I want to serve and be served consciously.

Fear

faer = peril

Many of us walk this world in fear, some to a greater, and others to a lesser, degree. It is one of the things that makes me sad about our planet. Fear is used as an excuse, a motivator, even a reason for choices we make. My favorite definition of fear although heterodox, makes it an acronym: **F**alse **E**vidence **A**ppearing **R**eal. We work hard to build a case in our own minds to justify our fear. Evidence-gathering is one of the most dangerous habits of humans. We can, with our magical minds, build a case for anything because we have the gift of consciousness, which means we can interpret our experience.

The original meaning of fear was *peril* or danger. Admittedly, there are those who truly live in peril, but certainly in the Western world, this is less rather than more common. So I think fear is really **F**alse **E**ducation **A**ppearing **R**eal. We learn fear, and we can unlearn it. The fallout of my childhood eye surgeries was that I learned not to trust, and even to fear, what I saw. Years later, I realized that the legacy I inherited was a felt-sense fear of trusting my own body. Time and experience in facing my fear has left me with a deep trust of my body and what I see.

If we were to take the time to look squarely and deeply at our fears in an effort to resolve them lovingly, I believe we could create peace on our blessed planet. Ask: How can I face fear and love it enough to heal it today?

Infinition:
Fear is part of the human experience and it no longer runs my life. Instead, I face my fears and I am set free.

Feeling

***felan* = to perceive**

Have you ever had a feeling about some future event that came to pass just as you felt it would? True feelings are not what we have come to understand as emotion. Emotion is more often our reactions to our feelings. My feeling on feelings is that there are four major ones, and if they don't rhyme, they don't count: sad, mad, bad, glad. All other feelings come under these categories.

The Anglo-Saxon root means *to perceive*. Feelings are more primal and less verbal than emotions because this kind of visceral perception is direct knowing. That's why we often name intuition as a feeling. I had plans to fly to Toronto years ago and the morning I was to go, I called my friends and said I couldn't get on the plane. It crashed on the way there. What I actually felt was dread in my belly; it was a bodily knowing. No mistake, that feeling is also the gerund form of the verb *to feel*, as in to touch. The feeling was palpable that day. We are inclined to dismiss our feelings as less valid than our thoughts. I think God gave us both channels for a reason. Ask: How can I honor my true feelings today?

Infinition:
I know feelings are simple and clear in their nature. I let go my reactions to my feelings and just allow them to be free.

Female

femella = a woman

In his *Dictionary of Word Origins*, John Ayto writes, "The symmetry between female and male is a comparatively recent development." So, what is it to be a woman? Just as with males, I think women (and men) spend their whole lives figuring this out. The deeper Latin root of *femella,* meaning *a woman*, is the verb *felare,* which means *to suck,* and was about nursing children. Yet, just as is so about maleness, biology is not destiny. There are as many types of women as there are types of men, and as many variations on femininity as on masculinity.

I am living proof of Carl Jung's theory of the opposite gender living as a force within the psyche of a gender. I experience my own masculine energy consciously. In women, Carl Jung called that energy the *animus.* In my lifetime, women have paid special attention to their *animi,* going out into the world, and doing far more than nursing children (although that's plenty!). What is this about? I think that gender fluidity is about becoming whole selves. Each gender needs to be able to call upon the other within itself in order to be fully functional in all aspects of life. Ask: How can I let go gender biases today and be free?

Infinition:
I choose to have all aspects of myself available to call upon when needed. I look at my feminine qualities as vital resources for giving my gifts to the world.

Flaw

flawe = fragment

Many of us consider our bodies or our characters flawed, and in fact, they probably are, but not in the sense most of us mean. The Middle English root of the word *fragment* gives rise to interesting psychological implications. We all know what happens when a glass shatters, but what does it mean for a person to become fragmented? We do just that—fragment ourselves—when we split off anything from our conscious awareness. What is split off becomes fragmented, and therefore fragile or, as the root of fragment itself implies, broken into pieces. You would think that fragmenting like this would be rare, but it isn't. We tend to split off whatever we don't want to remember. It can be as small a thing as a rude waiter or as large as emotional abuse. The more we deny and break off from ourselves, the more flawed or fragmented we feel.

My mother used to tease me that I liked life all tidied up in a pretty Tiffany box with a white satin ribbon. I do. I see all of life experience as valuable and not worth breaking off parts of myself. I'm certainly not perfect, but I'm not flawed, either. Ask: How am I fragmenting parts of myself today?

Infinition:

I am not perfect, and I no longer see myself as flawed. Instead, I commit to collecting the broken bits of myself and taking them to the Spirit Repair Crew Within.

Focus

focus = **hearth**

Focus is a Latin word which means, literally, *hearth*. In bygone times, the hearth was the center of the home. When we have focus, we are at home—in ourselves, with others, and in the world. I find it curious that the most recent flavor of the month in child psychology diagnosis is Attention Deficit Disorder, or ADD. Isn't ADD all about focus? Perhaps our children would be well served by our complete focus on them when we're together. I can't guarantee it, but I think it's worth a try.

Here is how to get focus. The definition of hearth is the floor of a fireplace. A floor is a foundation. And what is a fireplace? Obviously, a place for burning. Look carefully: a fireplace, or a place for fire. Spiritually, fire and its activity, burning, are representative of transformation and change. We must be at home, focused on the self, in our own centers, in order to let the fire of transformation have its wonderful way in our lives. The further message is that real change happens on the floor—at the foundational level of anything. Ask: How can I be at home today?

Infinition:
I am at home with my focus. It centers me so I welcome change gracefully. Let the transformation go on.

Forgiveness

for- = away
+
-gifan = to give

Forgiveness is the most selfish act in the world, but few people know this. It's actually a transliteration of a Latin word, *perdōnáre*, meaning *to thoroughly give* and the Anglo-Saxon makes the process itself clear. What we do when we forgive is *give away* whatever we were holding to ourselves too closely. When I forgive you, I set myself free and what you do or don't do is no longer of concern to me. One of the secrets of forgiving is to allow the right time to forgive to be revealed to you.

The story of Joseph the patriarch in the Hebrew Bible is famous for his words to the brothers who betrayed him: "You meant it for evil, but God meant it for good." Forgive, and then gently seek the message for your growth in the experience. And remember, forgiveness has its own right time. We make a mistake when we kid ourselves and forgive in the blush of intense feelings. The reason for this is that we can truncate our emotions and stuff them. We also make a mistake when we carry unforgiveness for too long. The reason for this is that we ourselves are the only ones hurt by carrying a long-term grudge.

Do your emotional process, and wait to hear that it's time to forgive. You'll know, I promise. Ask: How can I give away what is hurting me today?

Infinition:
I willingly forgive where I can: others, myself, and God. Where I feel unready to let go whatever it is, I wait and seek the right time to forgive. I am gentle with myself and others as I trust my own process.

Garbage

grabeller = to examine precisely

Well, here's an extremely everyday word, one we all have to deal with at one time or another. It seems to me that the only species which creates garbage is humanity. I've never heard of a pride of lions discussing what to do about the local landfill, have you? Interestingly, the Old French root of this word means _to examine precisely_, and isn't this what we are doing as we commit more and more to reduce, reuse, and recycle? Indeed, garbage becomes increasingly complicated in this day and age of recycling. The point of recycling as a discipline is to look genuinely at what we are creating as garbage and to make deliberate choices about how we use our resources.

I have a nylon shopping bag that zips into itself, which I carry in my purse. Because I use it nearly every day, I, by default, avoid using many plastic shopping bags. It's part of my commitment to how I deal with the garbage on earth. You've heard the expression, I'm sure, "One person's trash is another one's treasure." Take a moment to look at the things in your house. Do any need recycling? Do it. Circulation is the basis of prosperity in the universe. Ask: How can I examine precisely what I need and what I don't today?

Infinition:
I take a look at the garbage I create in my life consciously and I recycle what I no longer need so that it circulates and blesses others today.

Generosity

from
genus = kind

Humans are generous by nature. So often we think in eleemosy-nary (charity) terms when we think of generosity, but most generosity comes in simpler and humbler forms than million-dollar endowments to institutions. A flower. A note. A phone call. A cup of tea. It is the smallest moments in life that produce the feeling of generosity in people. I attended a birthday dinner for a friend recently and we all decided to share dessert. One of the guests commented, "You don't know what it is for me to share dessert." We all laughed because we knew what she meant. The truth is that it's hard to be generous when we don't feel that we ourselves are enough.

The Latin etymology is *genus*, which means *kind*. The root word is from an Indo-European base, *gen-*, which means produce. When I read that, I wondered if it was proDUCE as in creating things, or PROduce, as in lettuce? Then I decided it didn't matter. When what we produce is *kind* to others and ourselves, it is generous and it gen-erates more of the same naturally. Whether the produce is wonderful, healthy vegetables and fruits, or a helping hand, it's still generosity.

The spirit of generosity is engendered when we recognize that all of the inhabitants of earth are of the same kind, and we all benefit from random, and deliberate, acts of kindness. All. Ask: How can I be kind everywhere today?

Infinition:
I determine to live and act in a spirit of generosity at all times. I am kindness embodied and enacted, and my generosity brings gen-erosity to me.

Gentle

genus = kind

Gentle comes from a Latin word, *gentīlis*, that came to mean of high or noble birth; it also implied genteel treatment of those of "lower station" in life. Thankfully, this meaning has been lost as class-consciousness becomes less and less a factor in our world.

I remember being in the subway station at Second Avenue once when I was pregnant and seeing a devastatingly dirty homeless man. My baby kicked me at that moment, and I thought to myself that someone, his mother to be exact, had once felt about that man just as I did about my baby at that moment. Kinder eyes were mine as I looked at that homeless man that day.

A deeper meaning is to be found in another word of the same origin: *genus,* which means kind. It is normally used as a scientific word of classification. Kind. Yes, it's a classifier, and it's also a way to be with ourselves and others because we are all of the same kind. If there were one word I could give as a gift to the whole human race as a guideline for behavior, it would be Gentle. Ask: How am I the same kind as everyone else today?

Infinition:
I am gentle with myself because I am a part of all human*kind*. I am gentle with others because they are as well.

Goal

gaelan = to hinder

Motivational speakers the world over urge their listeners to set goals. I've done it myself. How will you know when you get where you want to be, I've said, if you don't know where you're wanting to go? I was surprised to discover that the Anglo-Saxon etymology of this word is *to hinder*. Thinking about it, though, it's true. A goal is an end point, a place to stop, and attaining one can sure impede forward motion. No point in running farther than the end zone for a touchdown. Has it ever happened to you that you've set a goal, worked for it, and have gotten exactly what you wanted?

Years ago, I thought I wanted to be a professional actress and when I left the theatre somewhat brokenhearted that was a goal I had to let go. Later, I set a new goal for performing. I decided that only the role of Kate in *The Taming of the Shrew* would make me go back on the stage. Well, I was offered Kate in a community theatre production and I took it and had a blast. After the show was over, I'd reached my personal goal, and I had a big letdown. I'd forgotten to make a new goal for my performing self. What I've learned over the years about goals is that I need them to be open-ended and flexible so that I don't hinder God doing what God does in my life. Ask: How can I be sure my goals bend to meet the real needs of my soul today?

Infinition:
I set open goals and I am just as willing to let them change as I grow. I let God work in my life and I usually receive better than what I've requested.

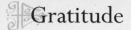# Gratitude

grātus = **pleasing**

Dr. Robert Schuller of the Crystal Cathedral recommends that we all cultivate an attitude of gratitude. I agree with him, but what about being grateful when we don't feel we have anything to be grateful for? Wonderfully, the one gift of God to humankind is free will, not free feelings. Gratitude is an act of will. I tell people who don't feel grateful to look at their hands. Most of us have ten fingers. Start on one side or the other and give thanks for each one. The point is: Start simple with what is closest.

I tend to think of the practice of gratitude as the flip side of what is known in Christianity as grace. Neither is dependent on the other, but both make each other easier. The Latin word root means *pleasing* and it's related to the Sanskrit *gürtá*, which means praise. We give gratitude naturally to that which pleases us, and it is a form of praise. Spiritual etymology would relate *grātus* to its homophone *gratis*, meaning free. Gratitude is an attitude free for the taking, should we so choose. God's grace is a free gift as well. Ask: How can I show what's pleasing to me today?

Infinition:
I take an attitude of gratitude easily because I am grateful for the gift of my life. I express gratitude to others and grace returns to me all the time.

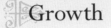Growth

grōwan = **to sprout**

Ask any farmer. Growth, as a process, is a mystery. Witness the farmer who planted carrots, and dug them up every day to see how they were progressing. Needless to say, the harvest was slim that season. Really, to grow, as its root tells us, is *to sprout*. Sprouting requires darkness, hence, mystery.

In the spiritual counseling which has absorbed my interest and time for years, I listen deeply to clients and together we make a plan to help them change and grow. We can and we must set our wills to our desired purposes, but then there comes a time when a mystical ingredient is added which catalyzes growth. That ingredient is God.

Our wills choose the seeds, and once we've planted them in the universe, there comes a time of waiting and wondering if sprouting is happening. It does, in God's Divine Order, and we will reap if we'll wait and trust the process. Remember Johnny Appleseed? Well, he didn't stick around for pie. Ask: How can I let the sprouting happen today?

Infinition:

I accept that how I grow is a mystery. I rejoice, nonetheless, that I do grow and my life shows me where I am growing and where I need to grow more.

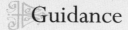Guidance

witan = to know

Part of the spiritual life is learning to seek inner guidance and *knowing* when it's right for us. What do I mean by guidance? It's help for making choices. Some of us hear a voice that guides us, some see visions, some get a visceral knowing. Guidance, though, can be a spiritual sand trap. Remember Shirley MacLaine in *Out on a Limb* losing her channeled tapes? She was relying too much on knowledge from outside herself. Here is the secret to avoiding the sand trap: Guidance, real guidance, comes only from within us. Only and ever.

Emilie Cady, a great metaphysical doctor, wrote, "Sooner or later, each must learn to stand alone with his [or her] own God." Guidance is between you and your God. Now, you may call it talking to the angels or the ancestors. That's okay. It doesn't matter what form you need; it matters that it's *your* guidance.

Here's what I do when I'm not sure I'm hearing correctly, or more usually, not hearing the whole message. I call a trusted spiritual friend and ask her to pray about my guidance and tell me what she gets. I know it's real guidance when I feel inner peace. Ask: How can I know that my guidance is real today?

Infinition:
I am learning to trust my inner guidance more and more every day. I am still and peaceful when I get guidance and then I follow it.

Guilt

gylt = a fault

I used to call this the "G word." Guilt. Purview of mothers of all nationalities around the world, also some religious institutions, businesses. You name it. Almost all of us have trafficked in guilt—either on the delivering or the receiving end. When my mother was dying, she had a stellar guilt day with me. When I called one of my brothers to get help in dealing with it, he said, "Refuse delivery." I laughed myself silly. Of course! Guilt, especially on the receiving end, is an emotional choice.

Its Germanic root *gelth-* means *pay,* and that's what we do. Usually when we accept delivery for something, we pay for it. Of note, the Anglo-Saxon has a slightly different spin. It means *a fault.* When we feel guilt, most often we are really dealing with blame we focus on ourselves. We *mea culpa* ourselves more than others do it to us. The easiest healing for guilt is speaking the truth. St. Augustine was right: Confession is good for the soul. Ask: How am I faulting myself today?

Infinition:

The moment I feel guilt, I look at what's causing it. If I'm blaming myself, I stop; if someone is blaming me, I speak the truth. I have a clear heart.

Habit

habitus = condition

from

habēre = to have

Habit has a pretty negative connotation for a lot of us, but in fact, habits can form supportive structures for an ordered life. When I get up in the morning, I usually run through the same routine every day. Ablutions; feed my cat, Charles; prayer time. I always find the toothpaste in the same place every day. The kitty food is in the same cupboard. My journal and rosary beads are in their usual spot. Habit is a support system if we set up our lives that way.

The deeper Latin root of habit is the verb *to have*, and a habit is *what one has*. Habits can be sustaining or draining depending upon how you use them in your life. Habit also means what *condition* one is in. So my question here is: What are your habits? Do you like them? Great. If not, or if your life needs a little waking up, change them. I can't get out of the bed on the other side because it's against a wall, but I could feed the cat before I brush my teeth in the morning. If your habits are unconscious, try going through them with awareness and see if you like your habits. Ask: How can I be awake to what I have today?

Infinition:
Habits can support me or sabotage me. I become aware and make conscious choices about my habits.

Happiness

hap = **chance**

The Declaration of Independence of the United States of America promises its citizens the rights to life, liberty, and the pursuit of happiness. I think the citizenry takes its rights quite seriously although I'll admit to wondering sometimes about where and how we choose to pursue happiness. To each his or her own. If we took a random sampling of people on the street, I wonder how many of them would tell us that they're happy?

The word itself tells us in a strange paradox that happiness cannot be pursued; that's not its nature. The Middle English root means *chance*. Happiness is chancy. It arises from what happens outside us, and depends on random acts. I think the founding fathers were telling us that we all have a chance at happiness if we'll pursue life and liberty for all beings. Ask: How am I relying on chance today?

Infinition:
Some days I'm happy and I celebrate that. On the days I'm not, I pursue life and liberty for all beings, and the chance to do that always brings me joy.

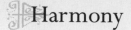# Harmony

harmos = a fitting

The quintessential musical harmony can be heard in a barbershop quartet rendition of "Sweet Adeline." Musically, harmony is an accompaniment to the melody. It's a wonderful metaphor for how to work with anyone as a team. Someone will always carry the melody, or be the team leader. When it's my turn to be a team follower, I take harmony as my lead. So I support, blend, and make the melody sound richer, better, and more interesting.

The Greek root word means *a fitting together*. Good harmony gives to the melody. I've always thought of the word team as an acronym: **T**ogether **E**veryone **A**chieves **M**ore. When my team experiences disharmony, we return to the simplicity of the melody and blend in again. Ask: How can I fit together with others today?

Infinition:

Sometimes I sing the melody in my life, and at other times, the harmony. I am a musician in God's ever-swelling composition and, together, we sound magnificent.

Have

***habban* = to hold**

Years ago I lived in a midtown apartment that had horrendous, old, old, old brown-sculptured carpet. To say that it was bad is to understate the case. So one day I got up the nerve to beard the landlord and ask for new carpet. What I wanted was pink carpet wall-to-wall. So, I visualized and called him to pop the question. To my delight, he said, "Sure. Go find the carpet you want, and I'll put it in." No problem. I went to the store and found exactly what I wanted in his price range and he ordered it. The rolls of carpet arrived—and we tripped over them in the lobby for eight weeks! What I'd been visualizing was asking for the carpet, not the carpet in the apartment, so that's what I got. Carpet, but not in the house.

The Anglo-Saxon root of this word tells us that to have something we need *to hold* it as our own. I wasn't holding the carpet for myself, so it took what seemed like forever to get it installed. I learned a valuable lesson which has been affirmed in weddings for time immemorial: to have and to hold from this day forward. When next you want to have something, hold it close. Ask: How can I hold close what I want to have today?

Infinition:
What I choose to have, I hold close to me today. I understand that having comes first from being, so I embody what I choose first and then the having is easy.

Hell

helan = to conceal

Remember that telling line in Belinda Carlisle's song, "Oooo, heaven is a place on earth"? Well, so is hell. And it's all up to us whether we make our own life experience a heaven or a hell. The Anglo-Saxon root is shared by the word _hall_ and it means _a covered place_. The word implies _concealment_, and our personal hells are places that are concealed. In fact, they become hells because they're concealed.

In the Sumerian myth, when Inanna goes to the Underworld to visit her sister, Erishkegal, she is stripped of all her queenly attire and left to enter hell naked. Later in the story, she escapes. Here is the secret to hell. If you find yourself approaching the gates of a possible hell, divest yourself of all pretense and face it nakedly. Tell yourself the facts as you perceive them, then follow the fifth step from Alcoholics Anonymous and tell one other person. Go to confession. The only way to grow is to face what is facing us—heaven or hell. Ask: How am I concealing from myself what I need to know so I can grow today?

Infinition:
There is no need to conceal anything from myself or from God. I face whatever is facing me and create my own clean slate.

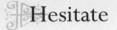Hesitate

hærēre = **to stick**

I'm sure you've heard it said that "the one who hesitates is lost." In some of us, hesitation is a learned habit. Shall I? Shall I not? What would be best? My astrological sign is Libra and by reputation Librans have a terrible time making up their minds. My usual experience is that some decisions are a piece of cake and others just aren't. If you hand me a complicated restaurant menu, no matter what kind of food, I'm likely to order a cheeseburger because I can't make up my mind. If, on the other hand (the four favorite words of a Libra), you want to know whether to take someone off life support, I can help with that easily.

The Latin root of hesitate means *to get stuck*. It's like having the front half of your car over a parking lot speed bump and being unable to budge the back half. If hesitation is a habit of yours, first decide if you like it and can live with it. Maybe you're just a deep considerer of all things. If you want to change your pattern of hesitation, try the obverse version of the adage, "Strike while the iron is hot." Begin to practice striking over sticking. You'll learn that whatever you choose can be chosen again if you don't like the results you get the first time. Ask: How can I stop getting stuck today?

Infinition:
If I feel a hesitation today, I honor it. There may be wisdom there. If I hesitate out of habit, I begin today to exercise my choosing muscles.

Holy

halig = sacred

I believe that holiness is the natural state of all beings. Hear the word _whole_ in holy. Spiritual etymology associates holiness with wholeness. We are all born whole, complete unto ourselves. Time, society, conditioning, karma all shape our souls into a place of less than full holiness so we spend our lives learning and growing into our innate wholeness.

In truth, the Anglo-Saxon root of _holy_ means _sacred_ or consecrated to God and Its purposes. This means that each of us has a holy purpose on this earth that is ours, and ours alone. Like snowflakes, no two purposes are alike. The meaning of this has a magnitude to it that staggers me. It would be ideal were we all born with a zipper pocket carrying our instructions for this life, but we're not. Our holiness is like a cosmic mystery novel in which each of us is the detective. Our inherent holiness, our wholeness, is what lets us seek and see the signs and miracles that guide us onto our right and perfect paths. Ask: How can I remember that I'm sacred today?

Infinition:
There is no doubt about it, I am holy. I have a consecrated purpose here on earth, and I am committed to seeking it while I find and complete it.

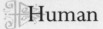Human

humus = the earth

As we begin the twenty-first century, many of us are lamenting just how disconnected we have become from the earth, our home. Dire predictions, wailings and gnashings of teeth, come from all directions. There are times when I certainly feel helpless to do anything to solve our burgeoning challenges, and then I remember that song from *My Fair Lady*, "On the Street Where You Live." That's exactly where I can do something for the earth. Whenever I go out, I make it a point to pick up the litter that I can on my street. Simple, and proactive.

On the level of consciousness, a simple solution comes from our own genus: human. Human is from the Latin, *humus*, which means *the earth* or, more literally soil, ground. This makes it easy to remember where we came from—the earth itself. Some of us have fond memories of childhood homes; some of us do not. Regardless, all of us come from the grandeur, power and beauty of the earth. Our bodies are made of the exact same elements as earth. Humans belong to the earth just as much as the earth belongs to humanity. Ask: How can I show that I belong to the earth today?

Infinition:
I celebrate my humanity by taking good care of the earth today for myself and all humanity. I remember and appreciate that the earth has taken very good care of humanity.

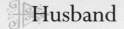Husband

hūs- = house

+

-bonda = master

There is a book on my shelf by an African anthropologist titled *Male Daughters, Female Husbands*. I bought it so I would remember that the roles we fill in our lives can be constraining if we don't do the work to define them ourselves. Social custom has a lot to do with what being a husband means. But what is it really? The Anglo-Saxon roots of this word mean *housemaster*. In some cases, this is certainly evident. But what about Mr. Mom?

Roles are important shorthand for interface in society. They make it easy to understand relationships between and among people. However, there is also room for defining for ourselves what husband means to us in our own relationships. I know lesbian couples and gay male couples who consider themselves husband and wife. I know others who do not. It seems to me that if a role we take on boxes us in, it is in our own best interests to define it as we need it to be. So if master of the house isn't your style, choose another. Ask: How can I fit my roles to me today?

Infinition:

The roles that I play make interaction and explanation easy. I am happiest with my roles when I define them for myself.

Idea

idein = **to see**

The entirety of creation is based on an idea. If you wanted to build a house, first you'd have the idea to build it, then you'd decide what you wanted it to look or feel like. Then you'd take your idea to an architect and have plans rendered, and only when the plans were as close to your idea as they could be would you hire a builder to put the house into form.

When you know that ideas are the true currency of the universe, the process of creating becomes much easier because you avoid getting caught up in the details of how. Think on this. The Greek root of the word idea means *to see*. You've heard it said, "I'll believe it when I see it." Now that you understand that the idea must always come first, you'll realize the error in that statement. The truth is, "You'll see it when you believe it." This means that all those times you spend daydreaming, visualizing, fantasizing are the times when you're creating using God's process most closely. See your ideas in manifestation, and then hire the builder. Ask: How can I see my life becoming today?

Infinition:
I understand the process of true creation. When I see my ideas first within myself, then manifestation is a breeze.

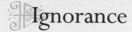gnorance

in- = not
+
-gnōrare = to know

Knowledge can be tricky. It's one thing to *learn* something—say, the multiplication tables or the principles of prosperity. It's an entirely different thing to *know* something. The difference has to do with our bodies. Learning is a brain activity. I can always tell you that the Battle of Hastings was in 1066 because my ninth-grade history teacher, Mr. Urie, drummed it into our skulls, but even though I haven't forgotten it, this isn't knowledge by a long shot. Knowing is a body activity because when we know something we know it in our cells, and at that point it can't be forgotten.

What it can be, however, is ignored. Ignorance comes from the Greek word *gnosis* for knowledge, and it means *not to know*. We may choose to ignore learning but we can't ignore knowing for too long without suffering. Ask: How can I stop ignoring what I know today?

Infinition:
Ignorance is not bliss; it's agony. Today I give myself permission to access all of the knowledge in my body. When I know, I feel great.

Illness

ille = ill

Somehow humanity has embraced illness as a normal and ex-
pected part of the human experience. Why? Think of other species,
like lions. They don't say to themselves that it's perfectly acceptable
to be unwell. I have a theory about illness that was inspired by some
words spoken by Swami Satchidananda: When we get out of the I and
return to the we, there will be no more sickness. Think about it.

Let's take as a working premise that all illness is foreshadowed in
our lives in some way. Namely, we are forewarned. A lingering, re-
peated headache. Recurring bronchial troubles. Soreness in a hand or
foot. What do we do with that piece of information? Some of us heed
the message. Others push willfully right by it, toughing it out. There
is a shame to being ill, at least in the West.

If you'll look at the root of the word, it could be read as the contraction for I will—*I'll*. Is it sheer stubbornness that makes us ignore
the signs in front of our faces? When a lion is ill, it returns to the
pride and seeks care. Are we to re-turn our pride from I Will (pre-
vail), and focus on the *We'll* of belonging to the community of life itself? Is it belonging to we that helps us let go of the I? Ask: How can I
let go my I Will and belong to my community today?

Infinition:
If I catch myself ignoring the billboards God is placing in my
path, I let go my pride and return to the community of life that gives
me care. I am wellness embodied.

Imagination

imāgo- = picture
+
-nasci = to be born

The word *imago* is used in entomology, the science of insects, to denote the final, perfect form of a specimen. Its deeper meaning is *natural shape* or *the picture of perfection*. An image is a *picture*—the natural shape of a desire in your mind. Walt Disney could be called the modern father of imagination. His cartoon mouse, Mickey, is a household image at this point. But he didn't start out as the Mickey Mouse that we know. He went through many different images before becoming what he is today.

Doctors who study the brain surmise that ninety-three percent of humans create what we desire from mental pictures—these are called visual people; the other seven percent use sound or sensation—called auditory people and kinesthetic people, respectively. The suffix *-nation* comes from the Latin for *to be born*. Our imaginations are the power behind being able to birth whatever we choose to see, hear, or sense in life. Look at it this way: Image A Nation. Ask: How can what I image in my mind be born today?

Infinition:

My imagination is part of what makes me part of God. I image my perfect life, and it is birthed in Divine Order now.

Impossible

im- = not

+

-posse = to be able

"Impossible!" wrote Oscar Hammerstein II, "for a pale yellow pumpkin to become a golden carriage. Impossible!" Just as impatient could be read, "I'm patient," impossible could be read, "I'm possible." The Latin roots of this word mean *not to be able*. Have you ever accomplished the impossible?

I used to work for a man who loved to challenge me with impossible requests. He worked all over the world and had a complete disregard for whatever time it was wherever I happened to be. So he'd call at 7 P.M. and ask me to find the exchange rate for Japanese yen to British pounds sterling at times when he knew nothing was open in New York. I'd put him on hold and ring California, where the exchanges were still open, to find the information. It always delighted him—and, I'll admit it, me.

The end of Mr. Hammerstein's song in *Cinderella* is, "Impossible! things are happening every day!" When Julie Andrews trilled those lyrics, she skipped the first exclamation point in her interpretation. Remember, with God, all things are indeed possible, and most especially you. Ask: How can I be more possible today?

Infinition:

I am so completely possible that it astonishes me. I live life from the God Spark within me and when I hear someone tell me something is impossible, I am happy to correct their misperception.

Incredible

in- = not

+

-crēdere = to believe

We hear this word all the time, usually in reference to the good things that occur in our lives. We call a friend to relate our good news and we hear back, "That's incredible!" The Latin roots of this word mean *not to believe*. Is that what we mean when we tell ourselves that something is incredible? I surely hope not!

If we repeatedly affirm that things are incredible in our lives, we will find our faith failing us because what we are really saying is "I don't believe it!" The greater truth is about ourselves. What we mean is that until whatever wonderful thing had happened in our experience, we weren't sure we could believe it might. Here is the place where doubt interfaces with faith.

The next time you're tempted to say to someone in response to a magical event that it's incredible, stop a moment, and check your faith thermometer. Then take a deep breath and say, quite calmly, "That's credible." You'll find the exclamation point disposes of itself. Ask: How can I allow magic to be credible in my life today?

Infinition:

The goodness in the world is totally to be believed, believed in, and credited to God today. I live a life full of magic and wonder, and it is indeed credible.

Infinite

in- = **not**
+
-finire = **to limit**

One of the most universal names for God is The Infinite. All religions can agree on this aspect of the nature of Deity. In a way, we really can't conceive of the infinity of anything, although I love that we even have this concept for contemplation. When human beings fall in love, part of what we touch on in ourselves is this connection to infinity, the notion that we are boundless and unlimited.

The Latin roots of this word mean *not to limit*. As a rule, however, humanity is adept at limiting itself. In fact, I might go so far as to say not only adept but expert. What if we were instead to remember that The Infinite is a part of us? When we limit ourselves, we think that The Infinite is apart from us, and here is the key. Watch yourself. When you meet a limit in your own being, face it and see what gift it has to offer you. I think you'll find that the limit was put there by you in another time and place and no longer serves you.

In your mind, draw a figure eight on the limit, as though it were a real wall. Now, set it on fire, and watch the figure eight turn itself onto its side. The eight, a mystical number of service to humanity, transforms into infinity and the wall melts within you. Ask: How have I been limiting myself today?

Infinition:
I am taking seriously the idea that I am truly unlimited and infinite by nature. When I find a place where I feel limited, The Infinite transforms me and I experience the infinity of the Divine Spark within me.

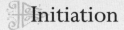Initiation

initium = **a beginning**

As part of my work, I create ceremonies for personal transformation. After years of doing this, it dawned on me that all ceremony is initiation. Interestingly, not all initiation requires formal ceremony. The Latin root of this word means *a beginning*. It can be any beginning.

I went to see a new ophthalmologist today; he told me that when people get to be over thirty-nine, things change in their eyes for the worse. This is where initiation is healing. I am certain that my eyes, even if I'm over forty, don't have to get worse. Not if I keep initiation and initiatory experience forefront in my consciousness. When we begin things, we have a reason to keep going. If I began to expect, like my eye doctor, that things will begin to go downhill now that I'm forty-something, then my initiation days would be over. Instead, I plan to stay young and vital during my whole life by participating in daily initiation ceremonies. Learn a new thing every day. Schedule a monthly outing that's outside your comfort zone. Stretch yourself in as many ways as you can to stay flexible. When you're always at the beginning, there is always something to anticipate with joy. Ask: How can I have an initiation today?

Infinition:
I welcome new things into my life. I stay flexible and young, and I enjoy broader and broader horizons.

Inspiration

in- = in
+
-spīrare = to breathe

There is an illusion in this world about creativity which needs disassembling. It is that creative people wait for inspiration, that their particular muse needs to show up before that poem, song, ballet can happen. Further to the myth is that inspiration strikes only the blessed few, not we who are average.

I am a mystery writer. The way I get my books done is, I show up at the computer, I exhale, and the words come. If we look at the word, it tells us how to allow inspiration to come to us effortlessly. The Latin root means *to breathe in*. Its original meaning implied the inflow of a divine agency. Have you ever thought about the miracle that is breathing? We don't think about it. It just happens. I studied breathing once and learned an amazing fact. It's not the inspiration that counts, it's the expiration. What causes us to breathe in *is* that we breathe out.

This is a perfect metaphor for creativity. First, we have to exhale all of what we thought we wanted to do, and only then can we inhale divine inspiration. Ask: How can I let go and breathe in today?

Infinition:
Right now I stop holding my breath, and I exhale like the North Wind. When I do, inspiration finds me and I am as creative as God.

Integrity

integritas = wholeness, untouched, entire

from *integer*

in- = not
+
-tangere = to touch

Self-enhancement teachers talk often about integrity. As the first level of the etymology indicates, it's a quality that bespeaks wholeness. Choosing, speaking, behaving from the wholeness within ourselves. Getting to integrity is often espoused, but seldom explained. I have actually asked a client a question and all the while his mouth was saying *Yes,* he was shaking his head—*No.* Classic out-of-integrity.

The word comes from the mathematical idea of the *integer,* which is a whole number as opposed to a fraction. The mathematical principle comes from Latin, meaning *not touched.* For me, living from integrity means living from the Divine Spark, what I call Spirit, within me. It is an untouched place of wholeness within me. Each of us was born with a natural integrity or, if you will, as a whole number. We learn to be fractions.

Visualize a big traffic light within your body, and here's how you get to integrity: The top light is between your eyes, the middle at your heart, and the bottom in your belly. To come from your own wholeness, ask yourself a question, then wait for all three lights to be green. Head, heart, gut all going in the same direction. Ask: How can I behave from my wholeness today?

Infinition:
There is an untouched place of perfection in me, my Divine Spark. I decide today to meet all of life with that Spark. Green lights abound.

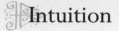Intuition

in- = **within**

+

-tuēri = **to look**

Tuition has come to mean the fees we pay to go to school in order to learn. Intuition means learning of another form—much less expensive, and far more dear (to use an old-fashioned word for expensive!). It means, literally, *to look within*, and is based on the idea that if we can ask the questions, whatever they may be, we can receive the answers from within.

Intuition behaves like a muscle, though: use it, and it strengthens; neglect it, and it weakens. This is not a case, however, of use it or lose it. We never lose our intuition. It is always present, patient, and willing to serve the good. I live my whole life based on my intuition—even down to the order of the errands I must run in a given day. I walk out the front door and ask if I should turn left or right. I listen and follow what I'm told. Invariably, some store is open that wouldn't ordinarily be, or I meet someone I need to see, or some other such synchronicity.

To live based on intuition can make life a wild adventure or a serene sail through calm waters of knowing—we who do it cannot imagine living any other way. Ask: How can I proceed with my inner learning today?

Infinition:

I trust my intuition to guide me infallibly. I look within to bring joy and ease to myself and others.

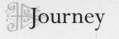

Journey

diurnus = daily

People on the spiritual path often talk about their experiences as being a part of a grand journey. The word endows the process with a mythological dimension. After all, a journey sounds so much bigger than a trip. Life lived on a spiritual basis is indeed a journey.

The Latin root of the word means *daily*, and you will recognize the French word for day as *jour*. Somehow journey conjures up mountains and valleys and heroic challenges, and the truth is that the real challenge is to live the spiritual life day by day. This means when someone cuts you off on the freeway, when your boss is cranky, when you're so mad you could shriek. In every single moment of every single day, and even when you fall off the spiritual wagon, climbing back on it. The secret to it is: Stay in the moment, this one, right now. Ask: How can I remember that my path is a daily one?

Infinition:
My journey is a day-by-day experience. I stay in the moment and I stay awake to my practice. If I forget, then when I remember, I return to the moment.

Joy

gaudium = a jewel

Joy is a jewel in the crown of the spiritual life. It is the result of living your purpose, loving everyone, and allowing the good to come to you. The most exciting thing about joy is that it's an inside job— meaning it comes from within us—and it's available to all of us no matter what is happening outside of us. I remember walking past a small shop recently. There was a sign in the window: HELP WANTED. INQUIRE WITHIN. My wordsmith's mind toyed with the words till they read: HELP WANTED? INQUIRE WITHIN. Here is where joy resides.

I see joy as a fountain that rises from the bottom of my spine and flows up through and out the top of my head overflowing to bless everyone I encounter. The key to experiencing joy is giving it away. The Latin root means *a jewel*. Giving out joy means living as a magical fairy tale witch with a treasure chest of jewels and giving them away to everyone you meet. The other day, there was a beautiful baby in my acupuncturist's office. I told his mother that her baby was as gorgeous as my cat, and she beamed. Another joy jewel given away. Ask: How can I give of the jewels within me today?

Infinition:
I accept joy as my birthright today without regard to circumstance. No matter what is happening, I am a fountain of joy.

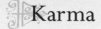Karma

***karma* = action**

Friends of my daughter have a new puppy and they named him Karma. When she speaks to them on the telephone, in the background can be heard, "Good, Karma! Good, Karma." And, "Bad, Karma! Bad, bad, Karma." This domestic picture illustrates the basic principle of karma, which is: What goes around, comes around. As I have written before, every choice has a consequence. In reality, karma, another word for consequence, is neither good nor bad.

The likelihood is that this word is derived from the great Hindu goddess, Kali Ma. Her name means Dark Mother. The Black Virgin statues in Europe signify the belief of the time that the dark mother represented matter. The Sanskrit base of this word means *action*. To quote Sir Isaac Newton, "For every action, there is an equal and opposite reaction." The greater truth about karma is that Spirit doesn't have any. It's only souls and bodies that play in the karma sandbox because karma only shows up in matter.

I have discovered that ninety percent of karma can be dissolved in three polite, quiet words: *No, thank you.* Try it, you might be surprised. Ask: How are my actions creating consequences today?

Infinition:
I choose to act in such a way as to enjoy the consequences of my actions. If I don't, I change my actions.

Kindness

cynd = **natural**

My father was killed in a plane crash when I was six years old, and over the years, the thing I have heard most often about him from people who knew him was that he was one of the kindest men they'd ever known. My brother, Frank, is very like him. The remarkable thing about kindness, according to its Anglo-Saxon etymology, is that it is *natural* for human beings to be kind.

I'm sure you've heard the Golden Rule: Do unto others as you would have them do unto you. Ever heard the Silver Rule? Do unto others before they do unto you. How does this work if kindness is natural? I believe that it is our belief in limitation that causes us to feel that if I have more, then you have to have less. In fact, there is as much kindness for each of us in the universe as we will claim—really, as much anything. Love, joy, peace, fun, you pick your pleasure here. It's easy to attract to ourselves what we want through kindness. Ask: How can I be especially kind today?

Infinition:

Kindness comes naturally to me. I am kind because I recognize that we are all of the same kind here on earth. Others are kind to me as a result.

Lack

lak = want

Remember that story of those days when I was broke? Well, one day I was singing myself a little prosperity song based on the Twenty-third Psalm, "The Lord is my Shepherd, I shall not want," which I'd just realized meant, "I shall not lack," and I decided to cross Forty-ninth Street in the middle of the block. At that moment, a bus heading west crossed my path. An advertisement on the side of the bus read: BORN RICH. In that moment, I got it about being broke. I was born rich! So were you.

The Middle English root of this word means *want*. Here's a spiritual secret: Your subconscious mind, where you hold your unconscious beliefs, is a willing servant. The only word it knows is *Yes*. So, when you are working at creating something in your life, say, a new job, and you say to yourself, "I want a new job," that obedient servant says, "Yes, you do want a new job." This is one of the reasons language is so important. We have to learn to say what we mean because the subconscious will simply agree with you. The better way to voice this, so your subconscious can help you manifest it, is: I choose to create a new job. Ask: How am I affirming what I really want in my life today?

Infinition:

I was born rich, and I lack for nothing. Whatever I want, I choose it, and creating is easy for me.

Language

lingua = the tongue

Language is the currency of relating, although there is so much more to communication than simple speech. The language of gesture. Body language. Tone. Pitch. Speed. Volume. Years ago, I coached ministers and taught master classes in what we called, in seminary, homiletics, or sermon-giving. Few ministers are taught to give sermons and fewer still are taught to give good sermons. My dear ex-husband, Antony, used to call bad sermons *snermons*, and I'm sure you know exactly what he meant!

The Latin root of this word means *the tongue*. There is great power in the tongue. Think of words spoken to inspire (as a good sermon ought!), words spoken to hurt, words to praise, words to wound. What you do with your tongue matters. I used to tell my students that if they wanted to speak thoughtfully, one way to encourage that is to keep your tongue in the bottom of your mouth in that little garage behind your bottom teeth where it belongs. Most of us go through life with our tongues on the roofs of our mouths—ready to talk at a moment's notice!

Instead, think, breathe, lift your tongue, and then communicate with all your various languages—words, gesture, body language, pitch, speed, tone, volume—with intent. Ask: How is my tongue a help to others today?

Infinition:
I am aware of the power in my tongue. I choose to use it and language to heal, to uplift, and to bless every day.

Lesson

lectio- = reading

There are many spiritual teachers who maintain that life is a school and that we are here to learn lessons. Personally, I think the homophone ought to come into play here. To wit, sometimes lessons lessen us. Besides, although I loved school, who wants to stay there forever?

The Latin root of this word means *reading*, and this is what I think we're here to learn to do—read the signs all around us. Part of my spiritual work with clients is that I create personal ceremonies for transforming difficult parts of the path. I have a big one coming up tomorrow, so I was thinking about it on my way home today. As I walked, I asked the Goddess for Her two cents on tomorrow's ceremony.

I took three steps north on West End Avenue, looked down, and saw two shiny, new pennies on the sidewalk in front of me! I burst into laughter, and got a message for my client. Not all signs make reading as easy as this one was, but the art of reading signs, omens, and portents makes living, as Helen Keller said, "a daring adventure." Ask: How can I learn the lesson of reading the signs today?

Infinition:

Lessons never lessen me. I am reading all the signs God is sending me every day. The more I practice, the better my reading gets.

Light

leukos = white

or

lux = light

G. K. Chesterton wrote, "Angels can fly because they take themselves lightly." To be light is also a powerful way of being in the world. Stuff happens, no question, but it's how we handle it that creates our experience. The Greek root means *white*, and the Latin root means *light*. White is, however, not the only color for light. In fact, add a prism to any ray of sunshine and you'll see the whole spectrum of light which we call, on magical rainy days, a rainbow.

When I first started doing healing work, I learned to send white light for healing. After years of practice, I find white light doesn't work for me. It can be too strong and too reflective. Witness those shiny days that aren't particularly sunny but make us squint anyway. What works for me is sending a rainbow, a gentler form of white light, more diffused which is far more easily absorbed.

Here's how to do this: When someone asks for healing energy or support to be sent to them, see in your mind's eye a rainbow in the sky. Coil it into a spiral and imagine it winging to support or heal your friend. See it wrap itself around her from bottom to top in a clockwise spiral. The rainbow colors she needs will find their way to her and the angels will take the others to become part of another rainbow. Ask: How can I treat the world lightly today?

Infinition:
The first thing God created was light. I need light for my well-being and I send rainbows of light to delight myself and others.

Limitation

līmes = **border**

When I directed my senior thesis project in college, I was given the option to present it in a black box theatre which could be configured any way I wanted it. I spent some time sitting in that space and couldn't get comfortable in it for some reason. That night, on my way home, I stopped into the chapel on campus. I could immediately visualize the piece in that space. Why? Because of the limits on the space. The doors were stationary, so were the pews. The piece was somewhat formal and it needed *borders*, as the Latin root of this word suggests.

I know spiritual teachers, myself included, who recommend limitlessness, and in absolute reality we are indeed limitless, but we live here on earth, where there are borders. Sometimes borders, like boundaries, give us a sense that we're safe. So while we feel that limitation can be, well . . . limiting, we can also be grateful for limitation which gives us a sense of well-being. The trick is to figure out which is which, and choose accordingly. Ask: How are the borders in my life setting me free?

Infinition:
I know the sky's the limit and it's all based on my choices. When I get to the borders of my consciousness, I ponder whether this is a helpful limitation or a harmful one, and I choose again.

Listen

hlystan = **to list**

Hearing and listening are two entirely different things. We all hear way too much—noise pollution is a definite danger these days. In fact, there are signs posted in Manhattan threatening a $150 fine for honking one's horn! Believe me, if the noise level is any indication, the city garners little revenue from their threat.

Listening comes from the Anglo-Saxon root word meaning *to list,* in the Leaning Tower of Pisa sense. Remember those E. F. Hutton television commercials? "When E. F. Hutton talks"—and the whole busy scene would freeze—"people listen." When we're really listening, we are indeed listing. Go to a restaurant, and watch people listen. Those who really listen will be exhibiting stooped or angled postures as they lean in toward the speaker.

Deep listening is an art to be cultivated. Mother Teresa has been described as someone who made everyone feel as though they were the only one. I aspire to this. This is a function of deep listening. Everyone needs to be deeply heard, and if we'll bring deep listening to our friends, our families, our co-workers, each one will feel precious. Lean over a little! Ask: How can I lean into what I need to hear today?

Infinition:

Listening is an art and I choose to work on my listening skills every day. I hush, lean toward whoever is speaking, and give them my full ear.

Longing

langien = **to lengthen**

Relationship guru Barbara De Angelis wrote a book years ago in which she described a hierarchy of emotions. To paraphrase, behind anger is always sadness, behind sadness is always fear, and behind fear is always longing. Indeed, longing can stretch a long way. The Anglo-Saxon root of the word means *to lengthen*. I think this is what genuine longing does. It, quite literally, lengthens our minds so we can expand to include whatever it is we're longing for in our consciousness.

When I was in seminary, I took a course in prayer techniques. Now, understanding that I had quite a reputation for prayer at the time, I didn't learn much in that class. In fact, I taught a lot of it. The truth about prayer is that it doesn't change God, it changes the one doing the praying. It lengthens our Spirits to include the desires God has put in our hearts. Let go any upset about what you long for, and pray! Ask: How can I lengthen my understanding today?

Infinition:
I understand that longing is put in my heart by my Divine Spark so I'll actually seek what I'm longing for. I pray about it today.

Magic

magus = sorcerer

The universe is a magical place . . . if we'll let it be. I first saw the musical version of *Peter Pan* when I was twenty-two. I'd never read the book or seen the Disney version. When Tinker Bell was dying, and she said, "If you believe in fairies, clap your hands," I was the first one on my feet, applauding like a maniac. I do, you know. I believe in fairies and elves, and good witches, and magic. I like my world this way.

The Persian etymology says this word means *sorcerer*. Yes, sorcery and magic are words that can conjure up scary images. But consider this: Magus is the singular form of the word Christianity recognizes as Magi, the Three Kings who visit the Baby Jesus on Epiphany with their gifts of gold, frankincense, and myrrh.

Still not convinced that magic isn't scary? Perhaps a homophone for sorcerer will make it easier? How about *sourcerer*? Someone who approaches life from its Source, or God. I think God has done some magical things here on earth. Look at the human hand. Look at the fact that grown-up pandas have only baby pandas (and never orangutans!). Look at the sun coming up in the east every single day. Magic can be seen by those who want to see it. Ask: How can I be a sourcerer today?

Infinition:
I live in the realm of magic and wonder because I live in God's creation. I choose to be part of the everyday magic and its Source.

Male

mas = a man

What is it to be a man? I think male people (and female people) spend their lives figuring this out. There are messages from their families, their peers, their society, which influence what it is to be a man. At the same time, at a soul level, there are messages that come from within each male about being a man. Carl Jung, part of the second wave of psychologists in the twentieth century, postulated that within each man was a feminine aspect to his soul called the *anima*.

The Latin root of the word male means *a man*. I certainly have known very feminine men, very masculine men, men who seemed to live between the two extremes, and all sorts of variations on the theme. At the bottom line, it seems to me that each man must determine for himself what it is to be male, and how that maleness works out in choices, behaviors, ideas, thoughts, dreams, and every other aspect of self. As the feminists of yesteryear so eloquently affirmed, "Biology is not destiny." This applies to both genders. Ask: How can I allow the male side of myself room to be today?

Infinition:
I know that all genders have male qualities and characteristics. I set myself free to explore them in myself, and to determine how I want to be as a male.

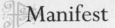Manifest

manus- = hand
+
-festus = gripped

Manifestation is a popular subject in metaphysical circles. People are always working on manifesting their dreams and desires. What does that mean? When something is manifest, it is *graspable by the hand*, according to its Latin roots. In other words, we can touch what is manifest. Some dictionaries imply that what is manifest is hand-struck, or handmade. What is it about the hands that is a key to manifestation?

Physically, your hands form a circuit similar to simple electrical circuits. Your hands are akin to the switch that activates the wires in the wall to make your lamp light up. The left hand is feminine and receptive; the right hand is masculine and active. We both give and take what we want with the right hand and we receive the results in our left hands, metaphorically (and no, it's not different if you're left-handed, which I am!).

Sit still for a moment and grasp one hand in the other. Which is on top? Usually, despite handedness, it will be the right hand on the top and the left on the bottom. Most of us think—it just feels right. Acting and receiving. Ask: How can I use my hands to grasp what I desire today?

Infinition:
Part of my task here on earth is to manifest what I choose. I use my hands as a metaphor to reach out into the world both to give and to take what I choose, and to receive it.

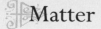Matter

māter = **mother**

Much of classical theology contrasts Spirit with Matter. St. Augustine, the saint I love to hate, (okay, hate is a little strong—how about . . . curse?) is the man I credit with single-handedly divorcing the body from the spirit. This is the greatest heresy perpetrated on humanity because it means we've lived in guilt for having bodies for longer than is decent. Spirit and Matter are two forms of identical energy. It's that simple. God created it all. All. Without exception.

Matter comes from the Latin root word *mater*, which means *mother*. The nature of God is both Father and Mother. God tells us in the Hebrew canon that we are made in Its image and likeness. This means that you can't be a father without being a mother and vice versa—and neither can God! I wrote my dissertation on the feminine in the Hebrew and Christian scriptures. In the first verse of the Hebrew Bible, it says, "God moved upon the face of the deep." In Hebrew, God is a masculine noun and the deep is a feminine noun. In the first verse! There's nothing the matter with matter. Ask: How can I mother the matter of my life today?

Infinition:
I know that if God is both Father and Mother, so am I. I can parent my whole life today with joy and ease.

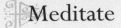Meditate

meditātus = **to revolve in one's mind**

from

med- = **middle**

Yes, I meditate and I believe everyone living a spiritual life ought to try it, and yet it's not for everyone. (Are you shocked?) There are many kinds of meditation. Classic meditation would have us all sitting in silence waiting for Silence to happen inside us. For some of us, it does, over time. For others, it never does. What to do? The Latin root of this word means to *revolve in one's mind*. Think on this. Doesn't revolving imply a center of some kind?

The deeper root means *middle*. What we're looking for in meditation is a sense of centeredness, of being able to approach life and events from the middle of our deepest selves. When do you feel the most centered? I know someone who goes to the gym to meditate. I know another person who runs in order to meditate. I know others who chant, some who light a candle. I myself sit in silence and have been doing it for more than twenty years. Experiment with meditation. Find what works for you and use it to increase your sense of your center. Ask: How can I come to life from the middle of me today?

Infinition:
Meditation is one of the tools on a spiritual path. I sit, I move, I sing my meditation in the way that is just right for me.

Meow

miaow = [echoic]

Strictly speaking, this word is not etymologically based, rather it is onomatopoetic. Meaning, it echoes the sound of itself. I am including it to stretch our minds to include languages other than written ones, and in honor of my sweet kitty angel, Charles. Pet lovers all over the world are daft about their animals. I'm the first in line. Having lived with a cat, I don't think I'll ever live without one again. We also maintain that our animals teach us all the time.

One of the most valuable things Charley Cat has taught me is, believe it or not, how to sit in a chair. When he sits on my lap, that's all he's doing and he's completely at ease. Feeling the total trust in his body as he sat, I realized that I used to sit in a chair ready to get up! So now, when I sit, I sit. I have a theory about Meow. We've been spelling it wrong all these years. (Cats, of course, do not deign to spell.) In reality, what kitties are saying when we hear *meow* is NOW. Charles never hesitates to speak up when he wants something. When I hear *meow*, it means, "Now, Mom!" Ask: How can I learn to trust the now today?

Infinition:
Animals are a precious trust to humanity from God. I take the opportunity to learn from those who speak many words, and those who have only one—but what a one!

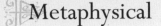Metaphysical

meta- = after or beyond
+
-physika = physical

I remember when I first discovered metaphysics. The idea that there even was anything beyond the physical was totally new to my mind, but I realized that I'd known the truth in my body for ages. The Greek word has a fun meaning. It comes from Aristotle's collected works, and means, literally, *after "The Physics,"* which was another of his treatises.

The principles of metaphysics underlie much of what is encompassed by New Thought and a lot of New Age doctrines. Included is the idea that everything has a meaning. Everything. Our task here is to learn both to look *beyond the physical* and read what we find there. Like this feng shui example: I've found that when there are plumbing problems in someone's living space, it can mean that something needs clearing out of the consciousness of the person. The pipes are only reflecting what is happening on the inside of the person! Ask: How can I see beyond the physical today?

Infinition:
I know that all events in my life have deeper meaning. I am committed to looking for each one and learning from it.

Miracle

mīrus = wonderful to see

There are theologians who would tell us that the age of miracles is over. It won't surprise you to hear that I beg to differ, and deeply. The Internet is full of mailing lists of people telling their miracle stories. All of us want to believe in miracles.

The Latin root of the word tells us how. It means *wonderful to see*. Miracles happen . . . when we see with wonder-full eyes. Interestingly, no one knows the etymology of the word *wonder*—and I've looked hard for it! I have a theory though. Say the word wonder aloud. What if its original spelling had been *one-der*? Bringing miracle eyes to anything means we see, as best we can, from a perspective of oneness. This means looking at facts until we arrive at the Truth behind them.

Here's an example: A diagnosis is not the same as a prognosis. Bring your miracle eyes, or, God eyes, to life. Watch for miracles. Ask: How can I see wonder-fully today?

Infinition:

I believe in miracles, and I know how to see them. I am determined to see everything in my life with miracle eyes.

Mood

mōd = mode, mind

Have you ever heard yourself say, "I'm not in the mood?" Moodiness is not one of my faults, so it surprises me whenever I hear this from others. Usually, we are referring to how we feel at a given moment. The thing about moods is that they're mutable, and change on a dime. One moment, we can be up and another down. What makes me wonder about all of this is that, since we have all experienced moods being so changeable, why do we take them so seriously? It makes no sense.

As the Anglo-Saxon root tells us, mood is all in the mind. It is the *mode of the mind*. We are in charge of our own minds! In point of fact, it is the one and only place we are in charge. I spent some time in an abusive relationship earlier in my life, and ended up at the mercy of the abuser's moods. The day came when it dawned on me that I could control my own moods, and that was the same day I knew I both could and would get out of what I'd gotten myself into. Ask: How can I work with the mode of my own mind today?

Infinition:
I am in charge of my own mind. When I feel moody, I take a look at its cause and then I happily change my mind.

Mystery

myein = to shut the eyes or mouth

Not only do I love reading mystery novels, but I write them as well. Good ones are like a challenging crossword puzzle. They require thought and persistence, and all the loose ends are wrapped up at the end of the day, just like all those squares are filled in. That's not the kind of mystery I mean here. These are the kind that aren't ever wrapped up and aren't ever filled in.

The Greek root of mystery is *to shut the eyes or mouth*. Its origin is in the Greek Mysteries, which were religious ceremonies of initiation. When we encounter mystery face-to-face, its awe can inspire shutting eyes and closing mouths. People who have had encounters with angels or near-death experiences sometimes wait years before they can believe enough of what they saw to begin to describe it to others. The soul of each person is just such a mystery. We can't hope ever to know its depths. Instead of facing mystery and trying to wrap up its loose ends or fill in its blanks, sit with it and be in awe.

As Trudy, the bag lady in *The Search for Signs of Intelligent Life in the Universe* recommends, "Take up awe-robics." Ask: How can I live the mystery today?

Infinition:
I am in awe of the amazing universe I inhabit, and I am comfortable with the mystery of life.

Myth

mythos = word, story

Jean Houston wrote a book called *A Mythic Life: Learning to Live Our Greatest Story*. For a long time it lived on the shelf near where I write. It's there to remind me of one of the great truths of life. We all write our own stories. Characters. Plotlines. Locations. The works. It is up to each one of us to choose the quality of the story. Paltry? Diminished? The Little Match Girl? Oliver Twist? Magnificent? Mythic? Aphrodite? Apollo?

The Greek root of this word means *story*, and it also means *word*. Your everyday words direct your story. Spend a day listening to what you say about yourself. Keep a list. What words recur? Are they uplifting and encouraging, or demeaning and negative? The quality of your story depends upon the words you choose and use. The best definition of a myth I ever read came from the mouth of a child, Annika Nelson: "A myth is a story who isn't true on the outside. But they are true on the inside." Ask: How can I tell myself the story I want to live today?

Infinition:
I listen to the stories I tell myself, and I choose to live the mythic life that is mine to live from now on.

Nature

nasci = to be born

Remember that clever, old margarine commercial on television? "It's not nice to fool Mother Nature." {SFX: thunderclap!} It's no mistake that we've dubbed nature a mother. (Folklorically speaking.) The Latin root of the word means *to be born*. At the very least a woman turned mother has to be present whenever a child of any species is born. Each one of us is born with our own nature.

I've heard people say, "That's just not my nature." I've always been curious about what we think our natures are. The words we speak when we own our natures tell us what we were born to be. Think of it. I detest large parties (I turn into the wallpaper). It's not my nature. I love small, intimate dinners (I get to engage with people in a real way). It's my nature.

We even call the wild places on our earth nature. Why do you suppose that is? Because those places, like the Grand Canyon, are what they are without explanation or apology. Many of us relate to God through nature. The greatest truth about your nature is that it is divine. Ask: How can I recognize my birth nature today?

Infinition:
I was born to be divine naturally, and so was everyone else. I recognize our collective rebirth as God today.

Need

nyd = compulsion

It has been said that God gives us what we need but not always what we want. To me, this has always seemed a spiritual trap. So, I need X dollars for the phone bill, and I want X dollars for a trip to Scotland, and that means God pays the phone bill but I have to skip the trip to Scotland? I can't get behind this, and so it interests me that some dictionaries use the word *want* as a definition for need.

The Anglo-Saxon root means *compulsion*, or must have. I think we get to decide on both—what we need, and what we want. The word compulsion means, literally, *with a pulse*. Something with a pulse has life. If we will put life force, energy, chi, pulse into what we both want and need, they become the same thing and we can have all that we choose. Ask: How can I pulse life into what I choose today?

Infinition:
My needs and wants are both legitimate because they're mine. I focus my life energy into both, and I delight in manifesting my life.

Nevertheless

never- = not ever

+

-the-

+

-less = not so much

Nevertheless is a compound word made of three smaller words. It is often used, along with the word regardless, by imposing and disapproving disciplinarians. "Nevertheless, young man/lady. . . ." Look at the word again with deeper eyes. Common English usage frowns upon the use of a double negative—"I Don't Get No . . . Satisfaction" *grâce à* Mick Jagger—and nevertheless is indeed a double negative. In mathematics a double negative equals a positive.

Let us look anew at nevertheless, literally, *not-ever-the-not-so-much*. Applying the principle of a double negative equaling a positive, now it means: Always The More. I find that I'm on the alert for my use of the word nevertheless in conversation. When I hear myself use it, I stop and iterate the real meaning: Always The More. I've seen it transform situations right before my eyes.

Interestingly, this is the word used in the King James Version of the Christian Scriptures before the most powerful prayer ever uttered. *Nevertheless, thy will be done.* Read properly: Always the more, thy will be done. Ask: How is the more always manifesting in my life today?

Infinition:
Never, never, never the less ever, ever, ever again! I always welcome the more into my life in all ways.

Nice

nescius = **ignorant**

from

ne- = **not**
+
-scire = **to know**

I remember a *New Yorker* cartoon of a man and a woman, clearly married. He is reading the newspaper and she is talking with a diabolical look on her face. The bubble over her head read, "Today I went to Cartier and got those sapphires I'd been wanting." His bubble read, "That's nice, dear." A sad comment on communication, I'd say.

Nice, meaning pleasant, is one of those words which over time came to mean its own exact opposite. Its original meaning was *foolish*, and it came from the Latin roots for *ignorant*. One of the keys to communicating effectively is deep listening. Another one is choosing our times to speak. When we use phrases like, "That's nice, dear," we are indeed remaining ignorant of what is really being discussed. Or, we are dismissing the subject and its speaker. I'm a believer in deep listening, and in asking questions if I don't understand the subject under discussion—after all, I might learn something!

Using standard phrases stifles real conversation. Next time you're tempted, ask an interested question instead. Ask: How can I show my interest instead of my ignorance today?

Infinition:
From now on I choose to stay awake in all my conversations. No more catch phrases for me. Instead, I show my interest and it's nice.

No

nān = none

There is a two-year-old who lives above me. Her all-time favorite word is *No*, spoken (and I understate the case here) at a pitch and a decibel that are indescribable. Her mother deserves sainthood and my halo is pretty shiny at this point, too. Still, that little *No* angel is teaching me something valuable.

I grew up at a time when nice girls said *No*, but very politely. In fact, I had to learn the power of *No* the hard way—by saying *Yes* when I meant *No* enough times that it hurt me. Then, believe me, I started saying *No* and meaning it in a really big way.

The Anglo-Saxon root of the word means *none*. It comes from a phrase: "I'll have none of it." There is no equivocating here. None means none. Not one. Not some. No, none. Not any. There is deep and abiding power in this word to draw boundaries and stick by them. One of the recognizable adages of feminist outrage is, "What part of *No* don't you understand?" A small word, but one that has great effect. Use it when you need it. Ask: How can I say *No* when I mean it today?

Infinition:
I know what my own boundaries are, and I honor them. When I feel the need to say *No* to something, I do it and I feel good about it.

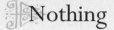# Nothing

nān- = none
+
-thing = thing

The Christian Scriptures quote Jesus of Nazareth as having said, "With God, nothing is impossible." It is of note that much of the scripture of the Middle East is written in the "negative." Read the Jesus quote again. It really means that, with God, everything is possible. Still, the negative version is more powerful. Why is that? Everything is almost too big a concept, but nothing is something we all understand. The candy jar is empty; I ate the last one. Nothing left. Interesting, isn't it, that we conceive the negative so much more clearly? Ah well.

The Anglo-Saxon root of the word means *none thing,* and, incidentally, we could read this as *no one thing.* No one thing, not anything I can dream up, is impossible with God. Nothing. What this means is nothing (pun intended) less than completely revolutionary! Dream it, and do whatever it is with God, and it's always possible. Ask: How can I make something from nothing today?

Infinition:

I remember that everything is possible with God so I give up the idea that I have to settle for nothing ever again.

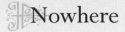 # Nowhere

no- = not any
+
-where = place

Customarily nowhere means *not in any place*. Here's a possible exchange between two business colleagues. Query: "How's it going on Project Q?" Response: "I'm nowhere." At different times in our lives, every single one of us has felt lost or like we're spinning our wheels.

The next time you think you are nowhere, look at the word again. For with a tiny shift, it solves its own problem and our dilemma. When you are nowhere, let the *w* shift its allegiance to give us all some guidance. *Now-* + *-Here*.

My husband and I wanted to move from the city to the country at one point in our lives. We affirmed that we were moving and packed boxes readying ourselves to go. It took us eighteen months and we missed a lot of the now here. In order to get from where we are to where we want to go, there's only one thing required—that we are now here. We might have moved sooner had we paid attention to this one salient detail! When we truly are awake to where we are in the moment, momentum is easily gained and so is progress. Ask: How can I be now here today?

Infinition:
When I feel like I am nowhere, I look around and get my bearings in an instant. Once I am here now, life is easy for me.

Obey

ob- = before
+
-audire = to hear

I was once in a production of *The Taming of the Shrew* and had the delightful opportunity to play Kate—the shrew herself. Remember, if you will, that whole play is about the activity of the title, namely, the taming of a shrew. Well, our young director was adamantly feminist and decided to make some minor changes to the famous speech in the fifth act called the Obedience Speech. Yes, the director (sorry, Will!) took the word *obey* out entirely! Today people take the word out of the traditional marriage vows as well. Why is that? What is our problem with obeying?

The Latin root means *to hear before,* and it tells us the real purpose for obeying. Obedience is really about a relationship with God, and our relationship with God is the only one that requires it. When we commit to obeying God, we commit to listening until we hear God before we act. I, for one, am totally committed to obeying. Ask: How can I hear before I act and obey today?

Infinition:
I am not afraid to obey God, for I know that God wants only the best for me. I listen, I hear, and I obey with joy.

Obligation

ob- = **before**
+
-ligare = **to link**

Society's norms and mores—or sometimes our own families—work to instill a sense of obligation in us. When someone gives us a gift, we often feel obligated to reciprocate. Just this morning, I spoke with a friend who is always fixing me home-cooked meals (since I refuse to cook at home), and I expressed a sense of obligation to compensate her in some way for her generosity toward me.

The Latin root of the word tells us what obligation is really about, and it means *to link before*. When there is a link of hearts, before anything is exchanged, an obligation is established. A healthy one—of giving because we want to give, receiving because someone wants to give to us, and giving again so we receive again. Some social and familial obligations don't feel like they offer us choice around hearts linking. So if you feel obligated, check your heart. If you find a genuine link there, celebrate your obligation. Ask: How has my heart been linked before today?

Infinition:

I give up all false sense of obligation. I am obliged when my heart is linked to the heart of another, and glad to fulfill the obligation.

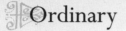# Ordinary

from
ordo = order

As a young girl, one of my greatest worries was that I would grow up to be ordinary—just an everyday, garden-variety, regular, normal person. I have to laugh now. Years later, after much mystical study, and hearing Divine Order much affirmed, I went dictionary trekking one day and looked up *ordinary*.

The Latin root is the word *ordo*, and it means *order*, a regular arrangement. Spiritual etymology tells me that the root of order is *os*, the Latin word for *mouth*. Divine Order is what God speaks into being. If you will recall the Hebrew Bible accounts of creation, God speaks the worlds into being. There's no memo, no meeting, no e-mail. Just words "Let there be. . . ." And there were. After that, ordinary . . . to wit, in the Divine Order of the Universe . . . didn't seem so bad to me. Ask: How can I celebrate the ordinary today?

Infinition:
I am aware that I am a part of the regular arrangement of the Universe today. With God, I speak order into my ordinary world.

Over

upari = above

I've said it myself at the end of a relationship. "It's over." What I've meant, of course, is finished, complete, ended. (Sometimes I borrow my lines from the soaps' writers!) Ending relationships is always difficult whether you are the breaker-up or the broken-up-with.

Interesting, isn't it, that the Sanskrit root of the word, *upari*, means *above*? Could this be what causes relationships to end? One or the other is rising above, or, to use another metaphor, deepening, where the other isn't. I believe that people are drawn to each other for the duration of the time when their paths are parallel and they promote one another's growth. If you ever hear yourself saying to your partner, "Get over it!," listen to what you are really saying. It's an invitation to come up higher and see things and yourselves from a higher or deeper perspective. Ask: How can I get over my own insistence on smallness today?

Infinition:
I take the God's-eye view of my life from now on. I see up and over the small, distracting details to the larger pattern of good.

Pain

pain

sounds like

pane

None of us enjoys pain whether its origins are physical or emotional, mental or spiritual, and yet the experience of pain is one of the bonding realities of humankind. Why do we all share this experience? I believe there is method in God's seeming madness. Originally, pain meant *penalty*. It comes from two Greek words: *tínein*, to pay, and *tímē*, price.

Herein lies the reason we all experience pain. We live under universal law without exception. It doesn't matter who jumps off the building; we are all subject to the law of gravity and there is a price to pay. Universal law comprises all those things which are always true all the time for everyone. Here's an example close to home. Try this: Breathe in, and hold your breath. Eventually, because of universal law, you will exhale. In fact, it is the exhale that causes the inhale. Believe me, there is deep pain when we forget to breathe.

Here is a way to handle pain: Use its homophone—*pane*. A pane is a piece of glass in a window, useful to look through to the other side. Ask: How can I use my pain, whatever it may be, as a pane today?

Infinition:
Today I see pain as my windowpane of opportunity for learning. I look at my pain with new eyes, and I am healed.

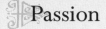# Passion

pati = to endure, suffer

We all want to have a passion in our lives—whether we admit it to ourselves or not. Passion for life is what makes it worth living. D. H. Lawrence wrote, "Genuine passions move you." The question is, where are you focusing your passion? Some people have a passion for their rheumatism. Others for golf. Still others, for their work or their families.

In order to reap the benefit of passion in our lives, we have to dedicate it to something. The Latin root tells us why; *pati* means *to endure* or *suffer*. Now, I'm sure you can imagine that I'm no advocate for suffering, but in this case it means *to undergo*. We do endure and suffer for our passions in life. They demand it of us. I have a passion for writing. I endure my time at the computer. (If only I had one I could talk to instead of type on!) It is the feeling of passion that allows us to endure being separated from a beloved. Passion itself is recognizable because it is enduring. Ask: How can I dedicate my passion today?

Infinition:
I decide to express my passion for life from now on. I dedicate my passion to whatever is worth my endurance.

Patience

from *pati* = to suffer

Patient is, of course, our name for a person under the care of a doctor. When it comes to some doctors and the subject of care, I myself have had the experience of impatience much more often! The root of the word is Latin *pati* and it means *to suffer*. Over time patience has come to mean to suffer without complaint. Surprisingly, the original meaning of suffer is different than we know it today. It meant simply *to go through* and didn't have a negative connotation at all.

I once heard a sermon called "I'm Patient"—all about impatience. The next time you are suffering impatience, think of St. Augustine. He said, "The reward of patience is patience." Wonderfully, the same root, *pati*, gives us the word *passion*. Patience is actually passionate expectation. Ask: How can I bring my passion to my suffering today?

Infinition:
Patience is indeed a virtue, and as of today, I count it among mine. I bring passionate expectation to whatever I'm experiencing and patience is easy for me.

Peace

pax = peace

I saw a bumper sticker on an old Volkswagen bus today that read: ANOTHER FAMILY FOR PEACE. It stopped me on the sidewalk. What family might that be, I asked? The truth is that until it's the global family we have to be content with one nuclear, VW bus-owning family at a time.

Although our word peace comes from the Latin *pax,* which means *peace,* its earlier antecedents are Anglo-Norman. The word is *pak* and it means *to fasten,* in the sense of *making something stable.* What needs fastening? It's simple. My heart to your heart, and yours to any other hearts you encounter, and theirs to . . . you get the idea. I am certain that there is only one way to achieve world peace and that is for people to establish inner peace in themselves. Once we do, we can give it away freely. Start today to establish inner peace in your heart. Ask: How can I bring peace to everyone I meet today?

Infinition:
I am deliberately fastening my heart to those of everyone I encounter from now on. I am committed to my own inner peace, and therefore, peace on earth.

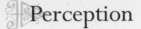Perception

percipere = to seize

Ralph Waldo Emerson wrote, "One hundred percent of reality is perception," and this is a one-hundred-percent truth. Have you ever heard a sibling tell their version of a family story only to wonder if you even grew up in the same family? This is perception. Ever had an argument in which someone quoted you to yourself and wondered if you'd really said that? This, too, is perception.

The Latin root of the word means *to seize*, and I think it tells us a lot about how our brains work. I can be in the same room as you and see the same event and we'll both see it completely differently. Perception is what we seize out of any given situation. The seiz-ure, if you will, is based on what we've stored in our brains already. If I hate olive green and someone in the scenario is wearing it, I will have antipathy toward that person based on my past programming. If you love olive green, you will be inclined toward sympathy with that same individual. The point is this: Perception actually involves choice. You choose what you seize. If, in some cases, you don't like what you got, choose again. Ask: How can I seize the best of my perceptions today?

Infinition:
I know I choose my perceptions and from now on I choose to keep the best and leave the rest.

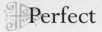
Perfect

per- = completely
+
-facere = to do

Here's a dangerous word: perfect. I learned a valuable lesson about trying to be perfect from my hair. When I was in high school, what was in (read: cool) was perfectly straight, hanging in the face, blond hair. It probably goes without saying that I didn't qualify on any front. My hair was naturally curly, did whatever it wanted, and I was a redhead to boot. I slept on orange juice cans to straighten my hair. I sat for hours under the dryer. One spritz of moisture in the air would ruin my "perfect" hair! It fascinates me now that people actually get their hair treated so it will look like mine does when I get out of the shower.

The Latin roots of *perfect* mean *to do completely*. Well, I did my hair more than completely and now my definition of perfect has changed. Funny how that works. I highly recommend that we give up the adjective PERfect and resolve only to use the verb perFECT. All of us are constantly perfecting ourselves, and as long as we are doing whatever we're doing completely, we're doing well. Being perfect isn't always the most interesting goal. Ask: How can I be about perfecting myself today?

Infinition:
I am aware of myself as a growing, perfecting being today. I give myself a break from having to be perfect—for keeps.

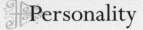Personality

persōna = mask

from

per- = through
+
-sonare = to sound

Personality is the vehicle through which we express who we are. We have a deep choice to make about our personalities. We can let them lead, and be guaranteed pretty superficial lives, or we can choose to use our personalities as a vessel for our spirit, the inner Divine Spark, which is the God Within each one of us. The Latin root of this word is *persona* and it means, literally, *a mask*. It refers to the masks that classical actors wore. In fact, the word *person* itself means *to sound through*.

It took me a long time to sift through my own masks. As a young woman, I tried on different sorts of personalities. As trial and error processes go, it was a lot of error (and a lot of cleanup) with plenty of trials. We've all heard the advice, "Just be yourself." I know I used to wonder, and just who might that be? The answer is easy when you choose to show your Divine Spark to the world through your personality. Just let the sound of God through the mask. Ask: How can I use my own personality for beautiful sounds today?

Infinition:
I know my personality is a tool for my Spirit. I let the Divine Spark burst into flame and I use my personality appropriately.

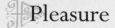Pleasure

placere = **to please**

There are psychological theories which say that our primary focus in life is all about avoiding pain and seeking pleasure; they also extend to life being about seeking pain relief and avoiding losing pleasure. I'm pretty sure it's not all quite as polar as this! So, the question here is: what's your pleasure? Do you even know? When clients come to me with a litany of what's wrong, I listen quietly for the most part and then I ask, "If your life could be any way you wanted it, how would that be?" In seventeen years of spiritual counseling, not one person has ever been able to answer that question. Never.

Try it for yourself now. What's your pleasure? The Latin root says that pleasure derives from *placere*, which means *to please*. Another, deeper meaning is *to calm* and from it comes our word *placid*, like a still lake. Let's translate the question now: What would calm you? Now take your pleasure, please. Ask: How can I pleasure and calm myself today?

Infinition:
Pleasure is calming to my Spirit. I take my pleasure easily today and every day. I deserve it.

Potential

potis- = able
+
-esse = to be

Butcher, baker, candlestick maker, chimes the famous nursery rhyme. Ballerina, Indian chief, fireman, artist, mommy, and the list could go on and on. What do you want to be when you grow up? I used to say, "A doctor," and at that time everyone thought it was cute because we all knew girls weren't doctors, they were nurses. What I was doing was reaching for my *potential*, from the Latin, what I am *able to be*.

For me, it turned out that I realized this particular potential; I am a Doctor of Divinity today (even though in those days I thought I meant a medical doctor!). Inherent in the word potential is the word *potent*, which means powerful, and this explains how God hears us when we discuss our potential. We are actually talking about *our power to be able to be* _____, you fill in the blank. Within potential is the power itself to realize our choices. Ask: How can I place my power behind what I choose to be today?

Infinition:
My power to become what I choose lies where my potential is. I choose my direction today and I let my potential power me there.

Prayer

prēcari = to entreat

In seminary, I earned the nickname The Promiscuous Pray-er—
she'll pray with anyone, anywhere, anytime. I still do. Why? Because
prayer is the only activity I've ever discovered which allows me to
contribute to any situation, no matter what. I can always pray even if
I can't fix something directly.

The Latin root is the verb *precari*, which means *to entreat*, and to
entreat means *to ask earnestly* from roots meaning *to treat inwardly*.
There is a further fascinating twist to this word based on the gender
of the Latin noun for prayer. It is a feminine noun, and one mystical
meaning of the feminine is the within. Look at the evidence: to treat
inwardly, and a feminine noun. So many of us think prayer is about
begging (sometimes called "storming the gates of heaven") or asking
the Big God in the Sky who is outside us for things we can't possibly
have without Divine Intervention, when in fact the word tells us that
prayer is about receiving and going within. Treat your prayer subjects
as something to take into yourself, to receive the guidance to know
what to do in every situation. Ask: How can I take prayer inside me
today?

Infinition:
I pray without ceasing and the more I treat the inward parts of
myself with prayer, the more answers I receive from within.

Prejudice

prae- = before
+
-iūdicium = judgment

from

iūs- = the law
+
-dīcere = declare

Prejudice has changed a good deal in the last four decades. In many ways, it's become a lot rarer, and in some ways, it's simply become a lot subtler. It means to form a premature opinion about someone or something based upon anything from gender to hair color, to a name, to a nationality. No matter what, prejudice robs us of actual life experience. To exhibit prejudice is *to declare the law* before knowing all of the facts. This is to say that we know what's right and that our own experience cannot, could not, and will not inform our lives.

For centuries courageous people have walked past this barrier. Consider Romeo and Juliet who, although fictional, faced the prejudice of their families. Rosa Parks faced the prejudice of race. Gandhi faced the prejudice of nationalism. I think the most insidious form of prejudice is the kind we don't even know is our own. I was walking in my neighborhood the other day and heard a beautiful gay man call another man a faggot in a cruel way. It broke my heart. Would that we could live in a world where prejudice were impossible! Ask: How am I declaring the law without knowing the facts today?

Infinition:
I listen deeply within myself today. Where I have prejudice, I let it go and open my heart to experience all the wonder in all of God's life here on earth.

Problem

pro- = **forward**
+
-ballein = **to throw, to drive**

In Richard Bach's masterpiece *Illusions: The Adventures of a Reluctant Messiah* is a magical handbook that opens to whatever you need in any given moment. One page reads: "Argue for your problems, and sure enough, they're yours." Do you ever argue for the problem? If you do, take a look at the etymology of the word problem.

The original meaning of the Greek word was *to throw forward* in the sense of tossing out a question for a solution. I've left the two different meanings of *-ballein* above, *to throw* and *to drive*, so we can understand the purpose of problems in our lives. Problems *drive us forward*. They are a form of creating both focus and momentum. Problems, as we name them so, tell us what to focus on and they move us in the direction of their solutions IF we'll let them.

The next time you perceive a problem in your life, stop, ask it two questions: Where shall I place my focus? How can I move toward a solution? Watch your "problems" dissolve. (That might read: re-solve.) Ask: How can my problems drive me forward today?

Infinition:

I give up having problems starting today. Instead, I choose to have focus and momentum because I'm interested in my life and how I live it.

Prosperity

pro- = before
+
-spēs = hope

If you've ever received a check from me in payment for something, whether you've provided me with a personal service or phone service, at the end of the line naming the payee, I write GIOS. I've been doing this for more than twenty years, not only when I write checks, but when I endorse them, and in that time only two people have ever asked me about it. GIOS stands for **G**od **I**s **O**ur **S**ource, and I write it to remind myself of the deepest truth about prosperity, which is . . . (drum roll, please!) that until all of us are prosperous, none of us is truly prosperous. When I write GIOS, I remember that God is my source just as much as your source or the phone company's source.

Everyone desires prosperity and the Latin root tells us why. Its deepest meaning is that for which we *hope before* the results we're seeking. So if you truly choose prosperity in your life, remember that it is a universal human hope, and choose it for everyone. Ask: How can I realize my hopes and help others realize theirs today?

Infinition:
I claim the manifestation of prosperity, whatever that means, for every being in the universe today. God is indeed OUR source.

Protection

pro- = in front
+
-tegere = to cover

The first time I did hands-on healing work as an adult, I worked on an actor friend of mine who had a major national commercial audition pending—and a sore throat. When he left my house, he was healed and he got the commercial. I was left with a sore throat for three days! Two days later a friend called and asked me to work on someone with lung cancer. I realized I had to get serious—and fast—about protection.

Some healers talk about using white light, but it's too intense for me. I learned to wrap myself in a blanket of rainbow colors before doing healing work. I used it for years. The Latin roots of protection *pro-* and *-tegere* mean *to cover in front*. I send my rainbow blanket before me into wherever I am doing healing work, so I don't take on whatever ailments my client has.

Recently, some nearly twenty years later, it dawned on me that I am divinely covered in front for as I do healing work, I am God's protégé, and I really have no need for any other protection. Ask: How can I recognize my divine protection today?

Infinition:
If I need protection from something, there is fear to look at in myself. I give up the fear and see that I am divinely protected all the time.

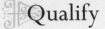# Qualify

quālis- = of what kind
+
-facere = to make

Salespersons qualify their prospects. One qualifies for a mortgage. We ask if someone is qualified for the job. When we qualify a statement we make, we add description to further explain it. The Latin roots of qualify mean *of what kind to make* of something. Qualifying has to do with noting the qualities of anything.

Let's say you want a new sofa. Sofa is a pretty broad category. Do you want a sofa, a davenport (as my grandmother would say), a loveseat, a settee, a sleeper? This is why salespersons qualify their prospects. In order to serve us, they need to know what we want, and more often than not, we arrive at the furniture store simply thinking "new sofa." Practice qualifying the things you are choosing to create in your life. Think. What kind of sofa? What color? What size? What make? What depth? What price? Look at those questions. They all begin with the word *what*.

Creating is much more efficient when we qualify the qualities we're seeking whether it's sofas or soulmates. Ask: How can I qualify the kind of qualities I choose today?

Infinition:
I take the time to qualify myself as a prospect for what I'm creating in my life today. I think on and name the qualities I choose.

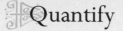Quantify

quantus- = **how great**
+
-facere = **to make**

I read in a business magazine once that of the workforce in the United States, seven percent of the people create things, and the other ninety-three percent measure the things the seven percent create. To me, that's a scary statistic. The spiritual truth is that everyone creates things all the time; we just don't always recognize it when we do. For example, this morning, I created a space in my life to sit at the computer and work on my book. I looked at my schedule and quantified, from the Latin roots, *how great to make* my commitment to writing today. My commitment to editorial timelines is quite helpful in this regard!

The point is this: it's up to you how you quantify both yourself and your life. How great do you want to make things? It's your measuring stick. Someone might feel really strongly about devoting her time to go to the hockey game. Not me. My measuring stick would rather stay home and read a book. Quantifying is the ability to decipher the amount of importance something has to you. Ask: How can I quantify my life so my priorities are in order today?

Infinition:
I am happy to create my own measuring stick for importance. I know what's important to me and I act accordingly.

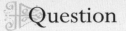Question

quaerere = to seek

I am convinced that the secret of living with artistry is to ask the right questions. Its Anglican root is the word *quest*, and here is the energy we need for asking the right questions. A quest involves the Latin root of the word *question*, which means *to seek*. When the Knights of the Round Table went on a quest, they were passionately seeking something, usually the Grail. When we have passion for seeking answers, it is the passion for our own questions that delivers the answers to us. Interestingly, at the end of the quest for the Grail, it is a question that releases its power.

The first time I saw the popular lapel button that reads "Question Authority," my wordsmith's mind read it completely differently than it was intended. It is supposed to read (aloud) "question AUTHORITY," and it's designed to make us think about that to which we give credence. What I saw was (say it aloud) QUESTION authority. And I thought to myself, "Who made you the question authority?" It's a good thing to be a question authority and I'll tell you why. It's only when we seek the questions with passion that we can expect their answers. Ask: How can I seek the best questions today?

Infinition:
I become a QUESTION authority about my own life. I seek the biggest questions, and I receive the biggest answers.

Rage

from
rabere = **to rave**

The original sense of this word suggests a fit of madness in the sense of lunacy, and this is what rage can do to us if we let anger become rage. Rage is the deepest form of anger. Anger, unexpressed, can become volcanic. In my experience, there are two forms of rage. The first is when we become enraged. This means turning our anger in on ourselves and stewing or seething till we create ulcers and the like. The second is when we become outraged. This means spewing our anger out on others, screaming or acting out till we create enemies and the like. Neither is particularly healthy.

I remember when I met my own unexpressed anger as rage for the first time. I was walking along the gorgeous Columbia River in Washington State with someone who totally infuriated me, and I began, as the Latin root suggests, *to rave* and rant at her. All of a sudden my arms were raised over my head as though I had a sword in them ready to come down on my friend and behead her. I realized it was the move of a Japanese warrior, and named my inner rager Samurai Babydoll. She had held the volcano at bay for long enough, and she went, as the saying goes, "stark, raving mad" for a while. Ask: How can I release my raving rage in a healthy way today?

Infinition:
Enraged or outraged, I choose to release rage and learn to express anger at the right person, at the right time, and in the right ways.

React

re- = again
+
-agein = to lead

As part of my spiritual practice, I seek the guidance of God on a daily basis. One of my favorite ways to test the guidance I get is to ring up a friend and ask for a gut reaction. I state what I heard, and I ask for her very first answer, not for thoughtful consideration. Usually gut reaction is accurate if you can catch it before your brain kicks in. We who live on a spiritual basis are encouraged not to react anymore, but to respond to stimuli that come our way. Because this is based on the radical judgment that reacting at all or ever is "bad," I don't think this is always the wisest approach.

The Greek roots of react mean *to lead again*. Reactions can lead us to inner truth in a lightning bolt sort of way. A spiritual teacher gave me a wonderful visualization that I've used for years. Picture a traffic light in your body. The three lamps, from top to bottom, are head, heart, and gut. She suggested we use it as an instant barometer for choices about taking action. Unless all three lights are green, don't go. Learn which of your reactions to trust and which to query. Ask: How are my reactions leading me to where I need to be today?

Infinition:
I trust my reactions, and if I don't, I check them out with other wise beings. I know my reactions can lead me to my truth.

Realization

rēs = thing

from

rās = riches

Many spiritual traditions place great emphasis on realization. Its standard metaphysical meaning is "to make real." Realization does make what we know real. This comes from the Latin word *res*, and it means *thing*, as in object of fixed property, or not imaginary. (Real estate is a good example.) When I was younger, I struggled deeply with my relationship with my mother. I felt it was a bottomless pit in me that I could never fill. Once she went to Hawaii, and sent me a postcard of a gorgeous, lush rain forest valley. I turned to a friend and said, "My mother went to Hawaii and sent me a picture of a hole." That was the realization that led to a turning point in our relating.

Interestingly, the deeper etymology of the word comes from the Sanskrit word for *riches*. What we make real in our lives does enrich us. God filled the hole in me quite nicely and my mama and I were good friends after that. Ask: How can I make real the riches of my inner knowing today?

Infinition:
My realization of my self is the most important task God has set for me. I own the riches of my being now. They are the real thing.

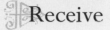# Receive

re- = back
+
-capere = to take

This is one of the hardest principles taught in the spiritual life. We have gone overboard in the giving department—waaaaay overboard, and taking "it is more blessed to give than to receive" to the proverbial nth degree, we burn out on giving and wonder why. It's simple really.

Receiving is part of an equation that follows the inexorability of mathematical principles. (Read this next bit twice.) The cost of giving is receiving. (Maybe I should write it again!) The cost of giving is receiving. What this means is: We cannot give without receiving, and the Latin roots of this word tell us so. They mean *to take back*. Here's how true giving works. First, we receive from God, and then we give. Next, we receive from God again, and give again. Ask: How can I take back to God what I've received so I may give again today?

Infinition:
Receiving is part of the divine equation of giving here on earth. I have this understanding in my cells from now on—first I receive, then I can give till it's time to receive again.

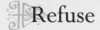# Refuse

refundere = to pour back

Recently two friends called to ask me if I wanted to attend an event at Madison Square Garden for a very worthy cause. I refused both invitations politely, "No, thank you." One friend asked me why, and I learned something very important about refusal. Most of us, in order to refuse an invitation comfortably, make something wrong.

My friend asked me why in a curious way, not in a challenging way. I was able to answer her that my idea of a nightmare is being in a 10,000-seat arena, no matter what the cause, unless I'm the one performing. I simply don't like it, so I refuse those opportunities without (and hear the homophone here) making them REfuse (read: garbage). We don't have to make anything wrong in order to refuse.

Simply take a cue from the Latin meaning _to pour back_. Something was poured for me that I chose not to accept. I poured it back to my friends so they could offer it to someone else. Ask: How can I refuse when I need to without making refuse of the original offer?

Infinition:

Refusal is easy for me because I know when I mean _No, thank you._ I let go of the need to make anything wrong at all.

Release

re- = again
+
-laxare = to loosen

Have you ever been advised to release something to God? Know how to do it? Many of us don't. And when we ask, few teachers can explain how. When we release a difficulty to God, we do exactly what the Latin roots of the word say—we *loosen* (our grip) *again*. Oftentimes, we hold too tightly to our challenges and magnetize more of the same to ourselves.

Here is a process that's worked for me. A lease is a contractual agreement, usually for space. When you re-lease spiritually, you write a new lease, a new contract, and since you're writing it, you can dictate your own terms. Write it for more space (around the problem). And now, let's take the word apart a different way. You'll know you've written the best agreement for you when you have re[a]l-ease. And that's release. Ask: How can I create real ease for myself today?

Infinition:
I loosen my grip where it's too tight today, and I release what I'm worrying about to God in me. I rewrite my lease, have more space, and feel real ease.

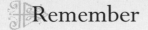

Remember

re- = again
+
-memoris = mindful

Lately, young friends of mine have taken to invoking the great god Alzheimer when they forget things. (Be careful what you invoke!) There are all sorts of reasons we forget things and Alzheimer's isn't the half of it. Stress, to be sure, is one major reason, although I think most of the reason is so that we actually make the opportunity to remember! Amazingly, Old French defines the word *member* as a part of the body. Do we ever forget and leave our hands and feet at home when we go to work? Not usually. Memory is a Divine gift to us all.

A few years ago, a dear friend of mine forgot my birthday. It came up in conversation about a month later, and although I was fine, she felt terrible. I told her that stress will do that to us—she was renovating a house, moving her office, and doing everyday life all at the same time! At the same time, something about me had been on my forgetful friend's mind. When she had the opportunity to remember, she was *mindful again*. Mindfulness is a state cited by the Buddha as awake. When we forget, maybe we're just asleep. Ask: How can I stay awake to all the members of my world today?

Infinition:
I am mindfulness itself today. I remember what I need to remember and I forget what I need to forget. It's easy to tell the difference.

Resent

re- = again
+
-sentire = to feel

I believe that resentment is the single most disastrous emotion for relationships in the universe. When people come to me to discuss their weddings, I give them all the same advice. If you're upset about anything for more than three days, get help. Call me, call a friend, or go see your therapist. Do something. The Latin roots of resent mean *to feel again* (we could add: and again and again and again), and that's what resentment is, the rehearsing and rerunning and slow-motion replaying of the same feeling (usually negative) over and over and over and over again.

Resentment unexpressed and, more important, unresolved, causes cracks in the foundations of our relationships. Mad for three days? Can't tell your beloved? Go tell someone, and figure out how to tell your partner. Better a brief sharp hurt—band-aid removal comes to mind here—than a long, slow rehashing and crumbling hearts. Ask: How can I resolve resentments I feel today?

Infinition:
If ever I fall into resentment, I get help in figuring out how to stop the instant replay and I take appropriate action to correct the upset.

Resist

re- = against
+
-sistere = to stand firm

Resistance is ninety percent of what causes us pain in our own personal growth. Resistance is like driving a car and gunning the gas with all your might whilst the other foot is on the brake just as adamantly. At its very root, resistance is the activity of fear. Fear is what causes us to make excuses, argue, obfuscate (look it up!), and generally make ourselves and those we love miserable, all the while protesting that we want to grow and change.

Ralph Waldo Emerson wrote, "What we resist persists." A perfect example: Whatever you do, don't think about the Statue of Liberty. How long did it take for her to show up in your mind? Emerson was right! When we resist, we *stand firm against* whatever it is that we really need to approach openly. Ask: How can I stop standing against what I need to embrace today?

Infinition:

Where I resist is probably where the greatest gifts lie for me right now. I cease resisting. I open my arms wide to the bounty waiting for me and am I blessed!

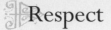

Respect

re- = **again**
+
-spectare = **to look at, regard**

R-E-S-P-E-C-T, can you hear Aretha singing? We all want it, and the fastest way to get it is . . . can you guess? . . . to give it. But what happens when we don't respect someone? A boss who cheats the company, even if only out of a ream of paper? A friend who gets extra change from a cashier knowingly and doesn't correct the error? A sibling who cheats at cards? It's not easy to offer personal respect where it doesn't seem warranted.

Showing disrespect to others only draws the same to us so here's what I do. I follow the Latin roots of this word and I *look again,* and further, I offer *regard again* to the cheater or thief without attachment. It's not my business to judge what other people do. I am responsible for my own behaviors. I choose to offer impersonal respect to everyone regardless of whether they merit it or not. It's the easier choice for me. Ask: How do I need to look again at what I'm having trouble respecting?

Infinition:
I offer regard and impersonal respect to everyone I encounter. It's simply the easier choice.

Respond

respondēre = to promise in return

As I'm sure you know, spiritual beings having a human experience are encouraged always to respond and never to react. I say, maybe. Sometimes the best response in the world is silence. A client called me once to say that she'd cheated on her lover. I said nothing. Finally, she sputtered at me something about me giving her Hail Marys or some sort of penance. I laughed, and told her that's not why she'd called me. She called to see if she would still be loved despite the fact that she'd cheated on her lover. Then she laughed with the sheer freedom of it.

The point was: What was she going to choose now? People cheat on their lovers all the time. What is your best response to that choice? So, X happened, and now, heeding the Latin root of the word, what Y do you want to *promise in return*? The best response is always a way to go forward from where you are to where you want to be. My client promised herself she would be true to her lover from then on. Ask: How can I best respond to what is happening right now?

Infinition:
I choose my responses consciously today. I ask myself what I want to promise in return to any happening, and I keep my promises.

Ritual

rīti = a going, the way

One of my favorite parts of private practice is creating personal ritual for deep healing and transformation. Ritual is the fastest way I know to create a full stop, to look deeply, to make new choices, and to change. For me, making ritual comes out of the Celtic tradition of *Wicca*, meaning wisdom. Sadly, much of the ritual is gone from our lives, and delightfully, this means we are free to create our own. The Sanskrit root of this word tells us why ritual creates change so easily. It means *a going* and implies *the way*, or a path out of where we start to get to where we choose to go.

A songwriter friend of mine had quit writing music years earlier, owing to some difficult events around her songs. When she came to me, she wanted her music back. After a series of ceremonies, designed to release the old, and invite in the new, I am thrilled to write here that she wrote her first of now many new songs! When you need an ongoing in your life, stop and ritualize the way you are going. The transformations can be truly miraculous. Ask: How can I stop in order to go on a new way today?

Infinition:

I know ritual is a crossroads place where I can signal a movement in my life onto a new path. When I need to step outside of ordinary time to acknowledge how I choose to change, I do it.

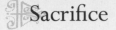# Sacrifice

sacer- = sacred
+
-facere = to make

When my son died, I read and reread the verses in Genesis in the Hebrew Bible about the sacrifice of Isaac. We had even named the baby Isaac. Here is what I gleaned. Abraham didn't have to sacrifice Isaac; the moral of the story is that he had to be *willing* to sacrifice Isaac. God, at the eleventh hour, provided a ram to sacrifice instead. There are some Biblical scholars who date the end of human sacrifice from this story.

I think what God is saying here is that nothing can come before our relationship with Divinity. Nothing. Not even our kids. When we are tempted to reprioritize, we are asked to make a sacrifice, and before you get bloody images in your mind, look at the Latin etymology of the word. When we sacrifice something, we *make* it *sacred*. We realign whatever our priority temptation is to the designs and purposes of the Divine Spark within us. While I was waiting for Isaac to be born and knowing all along that he would likely die, I sacrificed our Isaac quite deliberately to God. Another way to say this is: I gave Isaac to God and God's purposes in all our lives.

If you're tempted to edge God out in any given matter, consider making whatever it is sacred first. Ask: How can I sacrifice and make everything in my life sacred today?

Infinition:
I choose and understand my priorities in my life. God, self, beloved, work, in this order. If I ever get out of order, I willingly sacrifice whatever it is and see it made sacred before my very eyes.

Secret

se- = **apart**

+

-cernere = **to discern**

When I find the perfect gift for someone, whether it's for Christmas or a birthday, I love having a secret, don't you? I feel like a little girl about to burst with delight. This is the good kind of secret. In Alcoholics Anonymous, there is a saying, "You're only as sick as your secrets." These are the bad kinds of secrets, and whether they're about substance abuses, or any other kind of abuses, these are the secrets that burden us usually with shame.

The Latin roots of this word tell us how to heal the bad secrets. We need *to discern* (about the secrets) *apart* from our feelings of shame. Discern means to perceive distinctly—namely, we need to tell ourselves the truth about our secrets. Only when we do this step can we begin to discern ourselves apart from the secrets. As both the media and the Internet make our world more and more accessible to us, we are realizing that many of us share abuse experiences. The more we tell ourselves, and eventually, others about the bad secrets, the less bad they are and the healthier we are. Ask: How do I need to discern myself apart from any secrets I may carry today?

Infinition:

Discernment is a gift of true perception to me from God. If I can't see a secret clearly, I ask to see it through God's eyes. I see it clearly and I know exactly what to do about it.

Security

se- = apart from
+
-cūra = care

Oh, here is a whopper of a concept if ever there was one! People have stayed in boring jobs for security, in miserable marriages for security, even in religious traditions for security. Security is the reason my three siblings think I'm crazy for the way I live my life. The whole insurance industry is based on the illusion of security. Because—and I don't ordinarily consider myself an alarmist, but . . . there isn't any such thing! At least not as it's defined in today's world. The truth is that jobs can be downsized, marriages can end in divorce, and churches don't fall down when we leave them.

The Latin roots of this word give us much more security than our current (and in my opinion, narrow) definition. It means, literally, *apart from care*, not in the sense of uncaring or uncared for, but in the sense of carefree. AND, it's a choice. As long as we keep looking for security from outside of ourselves, we won't truly have any security. The moment it comes from within, meaning that it comes from ourselves and not others, we are carefree. Ask: How can I be so secure within myself that I am carefree today?

Infinition:
I realize that security is an inside job. If help is wanted, I inquire within, and I find all the security I'll ever need.

Shame

sceamu = shame

Oh, shame! Ouch! I personally think that shame is the most painful emotion. The reason for this is that we often have a hard time identifying the feeling in ourselves. This is partially because we naturally avoid feeling shame. It's so uncomfortable! Most of us play the blame game far more willingly; in my experience, blame is often shame projected onto others. What actually happens when we feel shame is that we have labeled ourselves as bad, even though usually shame is caused by particular behaviors. We globalize the message that our behavioral choices have been less than wonderful and apply them to our whole selves. So instead of "I did something bad," the message is internalized as "I am bad."

The Anglo-Saxon roots of the word go back to older still Scandinavian languages and mean, literally, *sham*. The inner experience of shame is that I am really a sham, a fake, not real. The subtext goes, "If you knew what I know about myself, you wouldn't think as highly of me as you do." Then the shame goes ever further and deeper into our souls.

To heal shame, start with this premise: God never made anything fake. God made me, *ergo*, I am not nor ever have been a sham. Ask: How can I feel truly real and alive today?

Infinition:
If there is shame about my past, I look at it right now. What's really a sham is the shame itself. There is nothing I can find out about myself that could possibly make me any less lovable—ever.

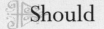
Should

sceolde = **I owe**

I'm sure you've heard the expression, "You shouldn't should on yourself." Talk about mixed messages! *Should* is actually the past tense of *shall*. When we say *I shall*, we really mean, *I plan to*. Somehow over centuries of usage, however, *should* has come to be the number one word we use to make ourselves and others wrong. Listen: "You should never have done that!" "I should never have trusted you." "They shouldn't have voted that in."

The Anglo-Saxon root has a deeper Germanic etymology that means, *I owe*, and this is exactly what happens when we use *should* in the way it has come to be used, especially when speaking to others. Do you hear the implication? You're wrong, is what we say, and now you owe me. Of all the words in common parlance, I think this is the one that (dare I say it?) asks to be expunged immediately.

Listen to yourself for a week. Are you a should-er? Look at that again. It isn't etymologically correct, but isn't it interesting that so many of us carry painful tension in our shoulders? Do you? If you'll listen for *should*, and begin to replace it with *could*, you might just find your shoulders relaxing. Ask: How can I let go of the feeling that people owe me today?

Infinition:
What I should or shouldn't, and what others should or shouldn't, is of no concern to me anymore. I switch should to could and I relax because I no longer owe anyone anything but love.

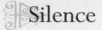Silence

dē- = from
+
-sinere = stopping

Just for a moment breathe in with me. Then, for fun, breathe out. Did you know that it is actually the exhalation that causes the inhalation? Once you've exhaled, you have to stop to take your next breath. In speech, we call this a pause. In music, we call this a rest. Silence is the same thing—a pause, a rest, and totally necessary to every single being on this planet although you'd never know it from listening. The noise here! It's deafening—so deafening that when, for an instant, we actually hear silence, it becomes even more deafening!

The Latin roots of this word mean *from stopping*. Stopping our speech, our music, our breath, our minds. Just stopping. But a lot of us don't stop. We barrel through our lives, full-tilt boogie all the time and wonder why we're so tired. It's from all the input. Silence is the best way to restore your energy and your perspective.

There is a hymn sung in Unity Churches called "In the Silence." It goes: "In the silence, there is a sacred place, a secret meeting place, God is there." I invite you into the Silence of your own being right now. Ask: How can I just stop and be silent today?

Infinition:
I know that silence is restorative. I make a place for silence in my life today, and as I do, I feel more myself.

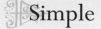# Simple

simplex = same-fold

At one time in my life, I was diagnosed with a chronic disease. Twelve years into the process, I heard the word simple over and over again like a mantra in meditation as I asked for guidance. I was seeing a massage therapist, a chiropractor, an acupuncturist, a doctor of Traditional Chinese Medicine, an Ayurvedic physician, an allopathic M.D., a gynecologist, and two surgeons, taking nearly forty pills a day, and feeling worse than rotten.

It took a while because simple is so simple that it's easy to overlook, but finally I got it. What I both wanted and needed was to simplify the whole regime. Fewer doctors. Fewer medications. Fewer procedures. Further meditation let me know which to choose and which to let go, and not surprisingly, my life got simpler as well. (And my health is now stellar!)

The Latin roots of simple mean *same-fold*, and come from a root meaning *single*. Imagine your life as a piece of paper. Isn't one fold easier than twenty? It is getting clearer to me that less is definitely more, and that simpler is always better. Ask: How can I simplify my life today?

Infinition:
Simpler is simply better. Where I have made things complicated or convoluted for myself, I make them single and simple from now on.

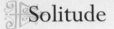Solitude

from
sōlus = alone

The Latin origin of the word solitude is, of course, *sole*, and English has several meanings for the word. Sole, as in *alone*. Sole, as in the fish. Sole, as in the bottom of the foot. And a homophone, soul, from Old French *seul*, meaning one. Such abundance! All of the meanings are germane here.

Someone wise once wrote, "Loneliness is solitude made wrong." This is where most of us get into trouble in relationships. We are born alone, and we must learn to be comfortable with ourselves when we are alone. This is where we experience our Oneness—when we are alone. Start by thinking of the soles of your feet. They ground you here. Were it not for these soles, you wouldn't be able to connect with the earth. Then think of fillet of sole (sorry to the vegans!)—it's the best part, isn't it? The center of the sole. And then a quick jump to soul, that which surrounds our Divine Spark, the gift of our Oneness in God. Now, I ask you, how can solitude (read: soulitude) ever be wrong? Ask: How can I be solely my soul today?

Infinition:
I am happy to be alone, in solitude, or in the company of others. I maintain my awareness of my soul solely by paying attention to the Oneness all around me.

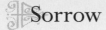Sorrow

sar = sore

Sorrow is sadness times a thousand. Often it is associated with grief, or prolonged sadness. When someone is sorrowing, their soul is *sore*, from the Anglo-Saxon, *sar*. Soul soreness is not as unusual as you might think. Sometimes people call it regret, or unforgiveness, or hatred, or resentment. Whatever its cause, the soreness can be unbearable.

When someone comes to me with sorrow, regardless of its origins, I recommend Sorrow Appointments. They serve the same function as gravestones in cemeteries. When you go to visit someone's grave, you don't stay there forever. You go, you visit, you do your talking to whoever is symbolically there, and you leave, knowing you can go back whenever you need to go back. The same with Sorrow Appointments. Make an agreement with yourself every day to do thirty minutes of sorrowing, and then leave it till your next appointment. If you'll do this for a few weeks, you'll be decidedly less sore because you've honored your sorrow. Ask: How can I keep my sorrow from becoming sore today?

Infinition:
If I carry sorrows, I set up my Sorrow Appointments right now for the next few weeks. As I honor my sorrow, my soul soreness is eased.

Source

surgere = to rise

An image from nature used for source is a fountainhead spouting water rising from deep within the land. That is where natural water comes from, so I ask, What is our source? Where do we come from naturally? My answer is that we all come from God. Each of us is a manifest facet of the source—God. As God is our source, we all *rise*, as the Latin root of source suggests, from godliness. This means that no one is born in original sin, and if you've ever held a brand-new baby in your arms, you know how true this is. I find it interesting that for centuries we have insisted theologically upon the fact that we are born "one down," if you will.

Look at the word source—do you see the word *our* in the center of it? Look at the Latin root for source—*surgere*—do you see the word *urge* in the center? Here's my take: God as our source is our urge to rise from Godself into the greatest expression possible. Ask: How am I recognizing my source today?

Infinition:

God is my fountainhead and I rise from this knowing into fullness, beauty, and grace.

Stress

strictus = **strict, narrow**

and

stringere = **to compress**

So here is the most notorious excuse for bad behavior in the book: stress. Actually, this is a shortened form of the whole word: distress. As in damsel in distress. (Just to be fair about it, I'd like to point out that there are plenty of stories about knights in distress as well.) At the risk of sounding like I'm metaphysically malpracticing, I truly believe that most stress is of our own making.

The Latin root of the word is *strictus*, which means *strict* or *narrow*. We decide on a goal and then we stress ourselves out trying with all our might to push the river to get there. Why? Instead, I think we'd all be better off and nicer about it if we'd decide on a goal, take steps to achieve it, and let go a little more. This is why. If you'll look at the deeper etymology of *strictus* from the Latin *stringere*, it means *to compress*. What we do is compress ourselves into smaller and more restricted spaces and timelines and wonder why we feel squashed, and then we call it stress.

Instead, how about an upgrade? Let's say we make a list of dreams for our lives, and then we stress (read: make more important) those that matter to us and let the Tao take care of the rest. Ask: How am I being too strict with myself today?

Infinition:
I give up distress totally today. Life will go on no matter what I do. I know when to make my goals important and when to let life lead me.

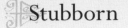# Stubborn

stybb = like a block

Okay, not to point a finger at anyone else, but I, for one, can be stubborn, especially about what I want. Not only that, but I can be downright fierce about certain things. Obstinate, obdurate, difficult, and generally a pain. I love the Anglo-Saxon root of this word; it means _like a block_. And doesn't that just illustrate exactly what happens when we're stubborn? We block our good (whatever that may mean to you) from manifesting in our lives by insisting everything happen the way we want it to happen. How many times have you set out to manifest something in your life only to discover that when you let go, something even better than you'd imagined came to you? For me, countless times.

Here's another way to perceive being stubborn: _born as a block_. One of the principles in Benjamin Hoff's _The Tao of Pooh_ is that of The Uncut Block. This means a block that has no particular form, but is formed by what occurs around it. The block goes with the flow, and its birthright to be no longer blocks its own good. The block follows The Way, the best English word for Tao. Ask: How can I unblock my own good today?

Infinition:
I can be stubborn, I admit it. Starting right now, when I am, I shift my focus to being the Uncut Block and let myself be shaped into the best me possible by the universal good.

Substance

substantia = essence

from

sub- = **under**
+
-stare = **to stand**

Substance is one of the most elusive concepts in metaphysical study. Aristotle wrote about a substance that is behind all manifestation. Some teachers have called it ether, and the mystics write about the ethereal realms. The original Latin root of substance means *essence*, and it comes from the deeper roots of *substantia* meaning *to stand under*. The substance of anything is its essence, what stands under any thing.

The easiest way to characterize substance is that it is the Divine Idea behind all other divine ideas. What stands under, or is the essence of, our entire universe is Divine Order—a divine idea of order. What stands under, or is the essence of, each person is the Divine Spark—a divine idea of Spirit. What stands under, or is the essence of, a table is the divine idea of a table.

All manifestation of any kind has as its essence an idea. So, let's say I decide I want a Queen Anne Victorian house. What is the Divine Idea behind that for me? Shelter, to be sure. Comfort. My own home. A dream come true. Divine Ideas stand under the essential manifestation of my dream house. If we begin to work with our lives at the level of the Divine Idea, things will come to us much more efficiently. Ask: How can I see what is standing under everything in my life today?

Infinition:
I traffic in Divine Ideas from now on and manifestation is play for me.

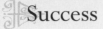Success

sub- = under or after
+
***cēdere* = to go**

Oh, illusive success! Here is one of the primary yardsticks measuring how we are doing in life. Are we successful? Whatever does *that* mean? First, please understand that despite the fact that we are taught that there are objective standards for success, there really aren't. Successes, and failures, are up to your personal determination, and only yours. Second, true success is based on your values. What do you value? If your answer is that it's time to write your novel, then a ninety-hour-a-week investment banking job, no matter the year-end bonus, is not really success to you, is it?

The real meaning of success, from the Latin roots, is *to go under*, or undergo. What are you willing to undergo for your success? Or, take the other meaning: in this case, *after*. It has to do with sequence. You go first, I go second, and I succeed you. Interestingly, the word tells us how to determine what success is for each one of us. Success is whatever we want *to go after*, what prompts us to contribute, care, and make a difference. That's success, and it's strictly personal, and immeasurable. Ask: How can I go after what I choose today?

Infinition:
I let go the world's definitions of success and really look for my own definition of success. Once I know what it is, I go after it with all my heart.

Sufficient

sufficere = to be enough

from

na = reach, attain

In 2nd Corinthians 12:9, St. Paul writes to the Christians in the city of Corinth these oft-quoted words from Jesus of Nazareth, "My grace is sufficient for thee." Is that your definition of sufficiency? The Latin root of the word means *to be enough*, and there is the Catch-22. What is enough? And how do we know? Usually we know when we've had enough negativity or noise or criticism, but otherwise we in the West seem to feel that more is always better. Not so. Friends of mine put their apartment on the market and sold it for their asking price, in cash, within three days. When they called to tell me of the sale, their first question was, "Did we charge enough?" Enough is up to you.

Enough is also variable depending on what you're measuring. Right now, I have plenty of clothes. Right now, although I have more than plenty of books, more books are always better. Right now, I have plenty of money, and more would be nice. See what I mean? The Sanskrit word *na* reveals a clue. You have to use your own sense of enough. Decide what's enough of any given thing, feeling, idea, then when you *attain* or *reach* it, it's enough. Ask: How can I determine and attain my own enoughness today?

Infinition:

Enoughness is completely subjective. I know what's enough for me in every area of my life. I know when I attain it, and it's enough.

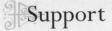

Support

sub- = near
+
-portare = to carry

All of us need and want support from the people around us, and we're deeply disappointed when we don't get it. Let's look at support from the other side, namely, how we give it. Do you give support easily and generously? What does giving support feel like to you? A lot of times support masquerades as commiseration, which isn't really supportive at all. Do you ever ask directly how you can support someone? The Latin roots of the word tell us that to support someone is to *carry* them and their concerns *near to us*.

An astrologer told a friend of mine that one January would be particularly difficult for her at work, and that she'd need a lot of support during that month. I started out to support her by leaving her an uplifting phone message every day. She soon asked me if it could be an e-mail instead, so I sent her an e-mail every day for thirty days, as she went through a huge transition, to remind her that she and her concerns were carried near to my heart.

The best way to get support, as always, is to give it—especially in the precise form the person needs. Ask: How can I carry someone near to me today?

Infinition:
I give support freely, and when I don't know how best to get that done, I ask. As a result, I am always supported.

Surprise

sur- = over

+

-prendere = to take

One of my spiritual daughters loves surprises. The other one hates them. I'm somewhere in between. When a surprise arrives in our lives, it catches us unawares. Surprises can be good or bad, but no matter which they remind us of how little control we have over just about everything. The Latin roots of surprise mean *to overtake*, and that's just what a surprise does; it takes over whatever the plan was, and supersedes it. There is a key to surprises, both good and bad, and that is to go with the flow and let the surprise overtake the plan.

Kenneth was a dear friend of mine who abhorred surprises, so when his partner threw him a surprise birthday party, he was furious and spoiled the party for himself and his guests. He had no regrets about his reaction either. When something arrives unexpectedly and takes over, for your own peace of mind, let go and let it. You might end up delightfully surprised. Ask: How can I let go and let the flow overtake me today?

Infinition:

Surprises happen and how I deal with them is up to me. From now on I choose to let the flow take over.

Surrender

sur- = up
+
-re- = back
+
-dare = to give

I think part of the reason we have such trouble with the act of surrender is that mostly we learn about surrender in the context of war, and therefore, we associate it with losing. I remember my brothers arm wrestling and crying out, "Uncle!" which meant, I give up. That's really what surrender is all about: giving up.

Most Westerners don't like giving up, but when we look at the Latin etymological roots of the word, we can see a deeper way to understand surrender. They mean *to give back up*. The *back* in between *give* and *up* intrigues me, particularly as it relates to spiritual surrender. Doesn't *back* imply that we're returning something which doesn't belong to us?

When I surrender, which I do daily, I look at it this way. Whatever I am surrendering, which is usually something that is causing me discomfort, I am giving it back either to the place where I got it, for it surely doesn't belong to me, or, I am giving it back up to God (and although I don't like "up" imagery for God, it's quite common) for transformation. Then it, and the discomfort, are no longer mine. Ask: How can I give back up what's hurting me today?

Infinition:

My white hankie is out and I'm a winner. I'm surrendering and giving back up what isn't mine anymore.

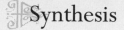Synthesis

syn- = **together**
+
-tithenai = **to place**

Political philosopher George Frederick Hegel set forth this tri-
adic construct: Thesis, Antithesis, Synthesis. One follows the other,
especially in spiritual work, like night follows day. Here's how it
functions. You start working with a prayer (thesis), let's say, for patience. Then like clockwork everything unlike patience shows up in
your life to show you where you need to practice it (antithesis). Then
suddenly you realize that you've become patient, and you piece together how you got there (synthesis).

The Greek roots of synthesis mean *to place together*. In this case,
we place together the desire for patience with all of our impatience.
Synthesis means integrating things that seem not to go together.
When I was in seminary, I was accused by my professors of being a
synthesist. I loved it! They didn't.

Much of spiritual growth involves placing together things that
seem not to go together and making not only sense out of how they
fit together, but synthesis. The more we can synthesize, the more
whole we are. Ask: How can I place together things that seem not to
go together in order to synthesize them today?

Infinition:
I am working with and understanding the delightful paradox of
synthesis. I am whole and free.

Thought

Gedächtnis = **memory**

"There is nothing either good or bad, but thinking makes it so," wrote that brilliant psychologist, William Shakespeare, in *Hamlet*. One of the oft-cited verses of the Hebrew Bible is that God gave humanity dominion. This has taken some quite devious and drastic forms over the years of civilization, and is lamented deeply by some of our more vocal environmentalists to this day. The mystical interpretation of that verse actually has to do with our thoughts. Oh yes, we were given dominion, but only in the realm of our own thoughts, not over other beings.

The Germanic root of thought is a word that means *memory*, and here is where dear Will comes in. Our minds record everything, and it is up to us to choose both what and how we remember our experiences. It is inner, mental judgments that cause us painful memory in this life. Take dominion over how you record your memories. This is not to say, don't remember the "bad" things. Do, and learn from them, but then take dominion and toss out the judgments. See how peaceful your mind can become. Ask: How can I choose what to record as memory today?

Infinition:
I take dominion over my thoughts today. If there are memories that cause me pain, I look at them, learn from them, and let go any judgments. My thoughts are peaceful.

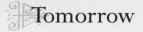Tomorrow

to- = on
+
-morgen = morning

Leaving a new love late one night, and knowing we had plans to see one another the next day, I heard myself, with a sense of anticipation, whisper, "Tomorrow!" The Anglo-Saxon roots of this word mean *on the morning*. Tomorrow can feel like a blessing or a curse. Have you ever counted the hours till you could see someone again? I have. Definitely a curse. I could have curled up with a good book and lost the hours of waiting. On the other hand, my whispered tomorrow felt like a blessing.

One of the best solutions to the way we experience time is the knowledge that there is and always will be a tomorrow. Yet we are best served by living today because we do not always know whether or whither we will be tomorrow. So at the same time as we anticipate tomorrow, if we live fully today, and when tomorrow becomes today, live fully that today, we stay in the present, where life is a gift. To quote Spencer Johnson's *The Precious Present*, that's why it's called the present. Ask: How can I live today fully and still appreciate tomorrow?

Infinition:

I accept the linearity of time as we experience it here on earth. I live fully today. I live fully when tomorrow becomes today as well.

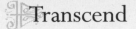Transcend

trans- = over, across
+
-scandere = to climb

Christian theologians teach that there are two major aspects to God: God Immanent—the God Within Us, and God Transcendent—the God Outside Us. Commonly pronouned as "He," I sometimes call Him the God of the Sunset, or the God of the Alps. He's the God that's always bigger than our problem, whatever it may be. He's the aspect of God worshipped exclusively in some sects of Christianity. The Latin roots of transcend mean _to climb over_, or _to climb across_, the idea being to get up over the difficulty and see it from a higher perspective.

A few years ago, I was given a teaching in meditation called the Matrinity made up of The Mother, The Madonna, and The Magdalene, which is a feminine version of the trinity. The purpose of the Matrinity is to heal Christianity of its historically demonized feminine faces for God. I was looking at the word transcend, and its etymology. Read this aloud to yourself: to climb across. Now read it a little more slowly: to climb a cross. AHA! The crux of much of Christian theology is the cross, and it is the transcendent god who asks Jesus to climb a cross. That very day my personal definition for transcend became: to end the trance (of only the Big Outside-of-Us God). Ask: How have I climbed the cross today?

Infinition:

I end the trance of the God outside of me as the only one. I climb over all my old, learned beliefs and find the Divine Spark within me. God and I rejoice!

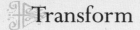Transform

trans- = across
+
-forma = form

The number of personal growth workshops and teachers that promise transformation through their work often surprises me. What are we so anxious to transform? And why do we think that this book or that workshop or this teacher will help us do what we can only ever do for ourselves? Oh sure, books and workshops and teachers can offer transformational clues, but when it comes right down to brass tacks, it's you and your God. Emilie Cady, a late-nineteenth-century brilliant doctor and metaphysician, writes, "Sooner or later each man [sic] must stand alone with his own God." (The same for women as well.)

When you desire transformation in your life, there is only one way to get it done, and that is to follow the Latin roots of the word itself. They mean *across form*. In order for true transformation to occur—matter-shifting and mind-altering alike—you must first take your consciousness across or against the current form you have chosen up to now. If you want better biceps, you can think about them all you want, and it would be good to pick up those barbells, too. When we want to change form, we have to go against what we've currently established. Ask God for guidance on how to get it done and help to do it. You'll be shown your best path for transformation. Ask: How do I need to go against whatever current form I want to change today?

Infinition:
I am my own guru for transformation. God provides all the answers from within me to make the changes I choose to see in my reality.

Truth

treowthu = **faithful**

Faced with the accusatory Sadducees and Pharisees in the Gospel of John, Pontius Pilate asks the famous question, "What is truth?" Oh, and do we love to bandy about our own personal versions of The (with a capital T) Truth (with another capital). In my understanding of how the universe works, there is no such thing as objective Truth. That's a dramatic statement, isn't it? Truth is relative to our experience, and only to our experience.

The Anglo-Saxon root comes from a word that means *faithful*, in the sense of steadfast or truing up. It refers to the strength in oak trees and how firmly they stand where they grow. Here is how truth works in our lives. What we believe to be true is where we place our faith. There is a Hindu story told of three blind sages who each touch an elephant. One says an elephant is smooth and hard. Another, loose and floppy. The third says, vast and massive. They are touching elephantine tusks, ears, and haunches. Each sage has his (or her) own truth. When we wield our personal experience of truth as a sword, we are unfaithful to the experience of others. Ask: How can I let my faith grow through the truths of others today?

Infinition:
I am truthful about my truth and I own that it's mine. The truths of others help my faith grow so I listen deeply and learn.

Uncomfortable

un- = not
+
-com- = with
+
-fortis = strength

A dear friend of mine had a skiing accident, which caused her to fall on her face. For months, she felt something just wasn't right. She kept saying, "I'm uncomfortable." It took a lot of searching but a doctor finally detected what was wrong, and now she's well again. What I noticed was that she felt weak almost the whole time she was looking for what was wrong.

The Latin roots of uncomfortable mean *not with strength*. Does this imply that when you're comfortable, you feel strong? Probably not like the mythological Atlas holding up the world, but yes, I think we do feel stronger when we're comfortable. (Remember, too, that sometimes what we don't feel is just as telling as what we do feel.) When I feel uncomfortable in a situation, I certainly don't feel at my strongest or most powerful.

Discomfort in any given circumstance is a message to pay attention. It's a warning that you're not at your best. Listen, and make whatever adjustments you need to make. Ask: How can I listen to the signals of strength from my body today?

Infinition:
When I am uncomfortable, I listen deeply to myself. It is a sign that I need to focus and see what I need to do in order for my strength to return.

⌘Understanding

understandand = to stand under

In the Wisdom literature of the Hebrew tradition, the Book of Proverbs quotes a father instructing his children in the importance of wisdom. In Chapter 4, he says, "Wisdom is the principal thing, therefore get wisdom: and with all thy getting, get understanding." This Jewish father is making a distinction between wisdom and understanding, and indeed, there is one. Let's look at a simple example.

I bought a new coffeepot the other day and was having a terrible time trying to get the proportions of coffee and water right, so my coffee tasted horrible. A domestic goddess friend of mine came to visit, took the pot, measured both water and coffee, and made two absolutely perfect cups of coffee. Then she taught me how. We both had wisdom. I realized I needed a new coffeepot so I got one. She knew how to figure out the right proportions—which in my book equals wisdom—and made the coffee. All the while she knew she'd have to teach me how, which definitely took understanding.

The Old English roots of understand mean *to stand under*. The best way to understand something, bar none, is to teach it to someone else. Then you'll know if you can stand under the wisdom you have, or if you can't, where you have something to learn. Ask: How can I share the understanding I have today?

Infinition:
I stand under what I know and share it when I can. Where I have something to learn, I am open and receptive. Then I gladly teach what I've learned to others.

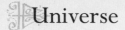Universe

ūnus = one

+

-vertere = to turn into

The universe comprises all created things. The planets, stars, plants, species, heavens, earths, everything. Do you live here? Sometimes I wonder how many of us do. There is, to my taste, a disheartening trend in some New Age circles having to do with "getting it right, so I don't have to come back here again." Sort of a mystical version of life as punishment for bad behavior.

As I understand the universe, which means from the Latin, *to turn into one*, we'll be in the same place no matter where we are, because there's only one place. This is why many spiritual traditions talk about eternal life. And why Jon Kabat-Zinn says, "No matter where you go, there you are." In fact, wherever you go, whether it's to California to find yourself or to heaven, there is still a soul called you that will be present.

The message here could be stated in a sweeter way. Until we learn to sing the *one song* that comprises the uni-verse, I think we get to return again and again in lots of different places for rehearsal. Then, once we learn to sing out, we can choose to take the vows of a bodhisattva, and return to help others learn to lift their voices as well. Ask: How can I sing the one song of the universe today?

Infinition:
There is only one place and there is only one song. We all live where we are and we all sing the parts we know. I sing out from now on.

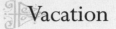Vacation

vacare = **to be empty**

I haven't been on a vacation for years, longer than I can remember, for the simple reason that I have no need to vacate my life. I like the way I live. I've chosen it deliberately, and I don't need to get away from it all in order to be restored. As I live it, restoration is built into my life in an everyday way. The friend who sighed to me, "I need a vacation," and heard me reply, "So we're looking to create a life that doesn't need vacating, right?" is partially responsible for the book you're reading right now.

The Latin root of vacation means *to be empty*, in the sense of *vacant*. This is not to say that I reject the idea of traveling or going on holiday, not at all. But going **to** something is far healthier than having to go **away** from something on a regular basis. If your life is such that you need to vacate it to be restored, be sure to include some time to be empty in your plans. Once you've emptied out a lot of what's stressing you, then it's time for holy days of curiosity and rest. Ask: How am I vacating my life today?

Infinition:
I choose to create my life in such a way that I don't need to escape it in order to be restored. In fact, my whole life is about days that are holy which include some empty time for me just to be.

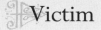Victim

weihen = consecrate

and

vice = in place of another

To be victimized is to be at the mercy of another, and it is not something that I would recommend for anyone. The Germanic and Latin roots of this word tell of its sacred origins. A victim was *consecrated*, and stood *in the place of another*. We have all had the experience of standing in the place of another and feeling victimized. Witness every theatrical understudy in the world feeling less than fully prepared.

Think of being a victim more personally. If someone you loved were threatened by violence and you happened to walk in on it, would you think twice about putting yourself between your beloved and the perpetrator? I am sure I'd be the first one to step between them—even if that's not the smartest choice according to the experts. My heart would act for me.

The point about playing the victim is that we don't have to stay there. Each one of us has been victimized in some way or another. The issue is: What do we do about it now? Do we stay the victim? Or do we shake it off, do what we have to do to process the experience, and go on with our lives? Ask: How am I playing the victim today?

Infinition:
I know that I have stood in the place of another in a consecrated way and so been a victim at times. I no longer reenact that experience and play the victim. I am the victor as I walk away from victimhood.

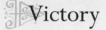Victory

from
vincere = **to conquer**

Everybody loves a winner, and everybody loves to win. Unfortunately, this often means there has to be a loser. There can only be one number one. The Latin root of victory means *to conquer*, which definitely has win-lose overtones even though we don't have to look at it this way. In recent years the phrase "win-win," which originated in the business community, has become popular. This is definitely an improvement, but I wonder if it's improved enough. What if we were to remove completely the concept of victory?

Conquer, which comes from Latin roots meaning *to seek*, brings a spiritually related word to mind, *concur*, which means *to run together*. I believe that the only win-win is to stop using winning as a way to measure success. Instead, let's take a cue from concur and run things together. That way all alliances are strategic alliances because everyone will win. Ask: How can I seek to run things together today?

Infinition:
I know I was trained to value victory, and I do, especially those victories when winning isn't as important as participating.

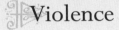Violence

violare = to use force

Violence is one of the scariest human experiences, if not the scariest. Having been in a relationship that included physical violence, I know whereof I speak. The hardest part of it for me wasn't being hit. No, that was easy compared to the realization that I had it in me to hit back in order to defend myself. It's not an easy admission, although I did retaliate in kind until I realized it was no solution to the problem at all. What I had to do was find help to get out.

The Latin root of violence means _to use force_, and force comes from the Latin for _strength_. There's a big difference and a fine line between force and strength. With violent behavior, strength is used as force. During that awful time in my life, I read somewhere, "In your vulnerability is your strength." That's when I began to understand that as I opened my heart to compassion for the abuser, I stood a much greater chance of getting out and getting better. It was three weeks from the time I read those words till I walked out the door a free woman.

Violence is learned behavior, and definitely not the best available coping skill. When you witness or experience violence, get out as soon as you can, and get help. Ask: How can I use my strength appropriately today?

Infinition:
I realize that we all carry the potential for violent behavior. If I have that tendency, I get help, and if I see it, I do what I can to stop it. I am strong enough not to choose violence.

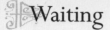# Waiting

wait

sounds like

weight

For some of us waiting just means *arrrrrgggghhh*. We want what we want when we want it—and that's final! Except . . . haven't we all had the experience of waiting for something and discovering that the waiting was just as important as the having of it? Like the last day of school? Or for that letter to come? From the Old High German, *wahta* originally meant *a guard* or *to watch*, as in *to lie hidden in wait*. Waiting ought to go with passionate expectation, and if it doesn't, some people manage to wait through its homophone: *weight*.

I know for me this takes two forms. First, when I'm waiting, I can feel a heavy sense of burden. Will the letter come? Will I be approved? It's a feeling of holding my breath about the future. Second, when I'm really waiting, I can gain physical weight. Eating to fill the time, and the empty place of fear about the future inside me. This can be a painful and unhealthy method. Tell yourself the truth about waiting and your weight today. Ask: How can I stop weighting while I'm on watch for my good today?

Infinition:
My weight is ideal for me right now, and when I have to wait for my good to arise in form, I use the time wisely, knowing that waiting means something good is happening even if I can't see it yet.

War

werra = confusion, strife

You know by now that I have a deep commitment to peace, and it would seem that war is its opposite. Well, it is, and it isn't. More often, I think that not-war is the opposite of war, and struggle is the opposite of peace. Another word for struggle is striving, the verb form of the Old High German etymology for war, *strife*. Much of Taoism is about non-doing, allowing, letting there be a way made clear for what we are choosing in life. I think the true genesis of war is confusion, and when we are confused (putting things together which don't go together), we struggle and experience strife.

It is my certainty that God did not create this universe as a place for us to struggle with or in, so why do we do it? Some of us don't feel alive unless we have an enemy, something which is "not a friend." Albert Einstein said that his bottom-line question was, "Is the universe a friendly place or not?" If it is, then the mud of confusion can settle in the roiling waters of strife, and we can, at last, live in not-war. Then and only then do we have the opportunity to choose peace. Ask: How is confusion causing me strife today?

Infinition:
I remember that the universe is a friendly place today. If I have perceived enemies inside or outside myself today, I let go my confusion and step out of striving into acceptance, and peace.

Whole

hāl = **healthy**

I had a client complain to me the other day, "I just want to be whole." The implication in that statement struck me as mammoth. The Anglo-Saxon root of whole means *healthy*, and the older Germanic root means *undamaged*. What my client was saying is that she perceives herself as damaged. Ouch! Upon reflection, I realize that many of us think of ourselves as damaged. Now follow my logic, please, and answer this question.

Who in you perceives the damage? There must be some part of you that is whole, healthy, and undamaged enough to perceive that there are some damaged bits, mustn't there? Of course, and that's called your Spirit, or Divine Spark. The next time you start to carp about your damaged bits, entertain my theory about human beings as icebergs. The bit of the iceberg we can see, that above water, comprises about ten percent. Sure, that bit has a few damages. And the other ninety percent under water minding its own business and doing just fine, thank you, is whole. Ask: How can I remember that I am whole and undamaged today?

Infinition:
Ninety percent of me is whole and healthy, and I'm working on the ten percent left damaged. I spend more time focused on the ninety than the ten.

Wife

wif = a woman

I remember the first time my husband introduced me to someone as "my wife, Susan." My brain literally went tilt in my head. Wife meant lots of things to me. I worked at home so I cooked, cleaned, ironed, shopped, and generally took care of daily reality. At dinner the night of our first anniversary, my husband said to me very gently, "Are you tired of playing house yet?" And that's exactly what I'd been doing. Arrrggghhh! It was my own learned ideas of what being a wife meant that I was acting out. I stopped that very day.

The Anglo-Saxon root of wife means *woman*, which means, in turn, *wife man*. Like husband, wife is a word which clarifies relationships. When women began to keep their own names rather than take their husbands' as a matter of course, we began to redefine what wife meant. Like the word husband, if what wife has meant to you doesn't work for you, think through what it does mean to you and choose that. Ask: How can I best be the person I was meant to be and in relationship with my partner as well?

Infinition:

I listen to myself deeply and I learn how I most happily define myself and my roles in life. I choose the most freeing definition for me. I am always my best self, on my own, and as a partner.

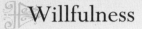Willfulness

wyllan = to choose

Oh, dear! Willfulness is not considered as particularly attractive or desirable. In fact, most of us find it distasteful, and yet . . . God's one gift to humankind is free will. Free will has a pretty bad reputation at this point. It is used to explain and excuse all kinds of unacceptable behavior, and in this, I think we miss the point.

Will is a gift from God and the Anglo-Saxon root tells us what we are to do with it and how to use it. We are *to choose*. How often we forget that we always have a choice! Always. I think we forget because we are not taught or encouraged to use our choosing muscles, so we're out of practice. Practice choosing. Look at a menu in a restaurant and in ten seconds, decide what you want for dinner. Choose whether to go left or right out your front door. Choose the black slacks or the brown ones.

Choose, choose, and choose again till your choosing muscles are limber and flexible. Once flexibility is attained, you'll never be willful again for it's when we don't feel like we have a choice that we dig in our heels, put on the brakes, and become obnoxious about having our own way. Ask: How can I do my choosing exercises today?

Infinition:

The best gift God gave me is choice. I'm showing my appreciation from now on by using my choosing muscles every chance I get.

Word

verbum = word

The Latin root of word is related to _verb_, what children learn as "action" words. Word has action implied in it. In John 1:14 we read, "The Word was made flesh and dwelt among us." In fact, our words are made flesh. What we speak consistently, we manifest by the implicit action of our words. This explains a lot about superstition, doesn't it?

I have a friend who, when she isn't interested in pursuing a line of thought, says, "Don't go there!" That would be my advice too, especially if you find yourself saying things you don't want to say and therefore don't want to choose. Your word is, indeed, your bond, and it can tie you up or set you free equally easily. Ask: How can I use my word to create the actions I choose today?

Infinition:

I know how powerful my words are in my life and I choose them carefully. I speak words of power, and I take the action to follow them to complete manifestation.

Work

ergon = energy

I don't know the exact statistics but I'm willing to wager that well over half the workforce in the West is miserable. To be honest, it makes me sad. How can we possibly spend most of our waking hours doing something we downright dislike? Yet, people do it. The Indo-European and Greek roots of the word work actually mean *energy*. Here is my criterion for work in my life: Does it give me energy or does it waste my energy? If a project gives me energy, then it's mine to do; if it doesn't, I don't do it.

Now, I know all the arguments about money and benefits and all those earth reasons for doing work we hate, but I can't imagine that God sent any one of us here to be miserable. There are millions of jobs here on earth, and we each have special talents designed to fill particular roles.

The true job is to seek and find our perfect work. Metaphysical writer Florence Scovel Shinn recommends an affirmation that speaks to this: "I do a perfect work in a perfect way. I give perfect service for perfect pay." Begin to sing this little song to yourself and ask for your perfect work. Watch for opening doors. Ask: How can I energize my perfect work today?

Infinition:

I devote my energy to seeking and finding my perfect work. I magnetize the ideal opportunities to me and I recognize them when I see them.

Worry

wyrgan = to strangle

I almost never worry. I was outclassed on the worry front so many years ago that it seemed useless to try to excel at something my mother was in charge of for the entire universe. My mother could even worry about worrying. So, at a very young age, I quit the worry cycle, and I'm glad I did.

The Anglo-Saxon root means *to strangle*. This is just what worry does. It strangles the person worrying. It strangles those worried about. It even strangles situations, circumstances, plans, and experiences. The technical process of strangling is depriving of air, and that's what happens when we worry. We literally deprive ourselves and others of inspiration. *Strangle* comes from a Greek word meaning *twisted*. This is what worry does; it twists current reality and future possibility so that we can't experience what is happening right now.

The best antidote for worry is breath—inspiration. Besides, how much of what you worry about ever comes to pass? Remember there is no such thing as preventative worry! Ask: How can I let inspiration enrich my experience of today?

Infinition:
I am through with worry starting right now. Instead, I let my breath untwist my fear about the future. I breathe freely and let tomorrow take care of itself.

Would

wolde = **wish**

Would is the participial form of the verb *to will*. Our wills are what we use to make choices in each moment. Often when we use the word would, we judge the choices of others based on our own values. We say, "I would never have done that!" What we do when we use the word in this way is express conditionality. Namely, we withhold our approval or love from others. Would is the second most common word we use to declare others wrong (the first is *should,* and we use this one most on ourselves).

The deeper truth of the matter is that we can never know what we would do until we are faced with that exact same situation, and then it's not what we would do but what we can do or are doing in that very moment. I got into tune with this word when I was recovering from an abusive relationship. People told me over and over again, "I would never have let that happen." The truth is, we can't ever really know what we always or never would have done until we're there.

Let's go back to the original meaning of would. The real meaning is *wish*. When we would that something were so (a bit Shakespearean, but so?), we wish for the best. Ask: How can I make what I wish for the world come true today?

Infinition:
I am tired of judging others, so I stop it today. Instead, I would ask that all good things come to all of us.

Yes

s$\bar{y}$ = be it so, let it be

Yeah. Sure. Why not? I guess so. Amen. Yes. They all mean the same thing in varying degrees. Why are there so many ways to say *Yes* in English? Because it's an affirmation derived from an Anglo-Saxon root meaning *be it so,* or *let it be.* If you'll listen carefully to conversation around you, you'll find that *Yes* is actually a little-used word. Instead, we seem to want to qualify it. I think it's because it is such a strong word. "Yes" can be a sentence all on its own.

Listen to yourself for a while. Do you qualify and water down *yes* when you use it? I challenge you to speak your *Yes* clearly and without qualification. What you'll find is that people will think that your communication skills have improved markedly. We all love to hear *Yes.* Ask: How can I use my *Yes* constructively, simply and clearly today?

Infinition:
I let my *Yes* be *Yes* and my *No* be *No* from now on. When I'm undecided, I don't hem or haw or qualify. Instead I am still until I know what I choose.

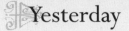Yesterday

geostran = yester
+
dœg = day

John Ayto's *Dictionary of Word Origins* credits the painter Dante Gabriel Rossetti with coining *yester* as a word unto itself, as in yester-year. Yesterday was a word by the time of Old English codification. I think it's a magical word because it points our focus right where it belongs as I see it: *yes-to-today*. "Yesterday is history," goes the beginning of a axiom on mindfulness. If we can learn from it, let's do it, and get on with life. Here's the rest of the axiom: Tomorrow's a mystery. Today is a gift—that's why it's called the present.

An artist coined this word, and I am content to end this edition of *God's Dictionary* with the reminder inherent in an artist's life. Living life is indeed the art of leaving yesterday behind, letting tomorrow be a mystery, and gifting ourselves with the present of the present. After all, that's exactly how creation works. Ask: How can I say *Yes* to the gift of life today?

Infinition:

I am an artist in my own right. I create my own life as my *magnum opus*, and I am fulfilled beyond my wildest imaginings.

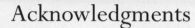

Acknowledgments

The picture of the lonely writer slogging away at her computer holds true for the initial penning of the work, but oh my! it changes as soon as one other person gets to hear or read the first word. I have been helped by more spirits than I can count in the writing of *God's Dictionary*. I name and thank abundantly:

> Richard J. Bartlett, website genius halfway across
> the world
> Richard Beeson, word wizard and soulmate
> Stephanie Blackwood, generous giver of valuable
> early feedback
> Lucia Mabel Mooney Burton, one-room school-
> house teacher and great-grandmother
> Kenneth B. Calkins, best friend who teased me

about *Miss Susan's Spiritual Lexicon* forever; I wish that he were here to read it in the flesh

Theodore Steinway Chapin, lifetime mentor, friend, and champion

Lonnie Coplen, always interested and always supportive, near or far

Antony Corso, first and best ex-husband, who named me "Miss Word" years ago

Isaac Stephen Corso, the son who made me who I am today

Christian de la Huerta, wise shaman advisor and founder of Q-Spirit, in whose quarterly newsletter I have a column called "The Word Witch"

M. Stephen Falk—Daddy, whom I miss every day

Joel Fotinos, soul friend and book maven *non pareil*

Dorothy Frye, proofreader *extraordinaire*

Elli Frye, shining muse, and receiver of each and every word hot off the press

Ashala Gabriel, blessed agent and advocate

Dr. Joseph A. Garduno, dean of The College of Divine Metaphysics

Patricia A. Gift, fairy godmother and definitely a gift

Christopher Goffredo, the friend always willing to go deeper

Linda S. Golding, wise counselor and strategist

Frances Goodwin, sister Libra, healer of healers, word wonderer in her own right

Ricky Grapp, teacher of my spirit, soul and body

Nicole Harman, number one cheerleader from the day we met

Paul Harman, gentleman, scholar, baritone, and knight in shining armor

Jacqueline Hobbs, goblin daughter *par excellence*

Lucia Burton Jackson, grandmother and childhood favorite

Debbie Luican, media wizard and sage stalwart presence

Mark Matousek, author and helpful navigator through treacherous waters

M. Kilburg Reedy, attorney-at-law and trademark traveler

David Tochterman, manager and friend

Virginia Waters, Ph.D., keeper of the sacred cauldron of sanity

Rona Wilk, daughter of constancy and operatic drama and delight

Linda "Amelia" Jackson Williams, my best mom—I miss her every single day

M. E. Zuba, former Chief of Security

I bow to and thank the thousands of clients who have entrusted me to walk parallel with them for a time in their spiritual lives. Many of them have been in recovery. There are references to the "Anonymous" programs in *God's Dictionary*. I am grateful these programs exist for they have saved the lives of many with whom I have been privileged to work.

I thank all those who participate in Sanctuary, the online omni-faith community of which I am the spiritual leader. Please join us at www.sanctuarycommunity.org. I am grateful to those who support "Seeds for Sanctuary," my weekly e-newsletter of spiritual inspiration. (If you'd like to be added to the list, e-mail NYCSanctus@aol.com.)

To the tightly knit crew at Tarcher, there are not enough kudos in the world! Sue Andrews, proofreader; Sara Carder, editor; Amanda Dewey, designer; Joel Fotinos, publisher and friend; Kelly Groves, publicist; Timothy Meyer, production editor; Ken Siman, publicist and friend, Toby Yuen, copyeditor, and the all-star sales force, I am deeply grateful.

Best for last: overflowing and eternal gratitude to God, Goddess, the Mother of All, the Father of All, and the Whole/Holy Divine Spark of inspiration within each one of us.

About the Author

Dr. Susan Corso is an ordained, omni-faith minister with a Doctorate in Divinity, an author, a columnist, a lyricist, a peaceworker, a spiritual counselor, a healer, a ceremonialist, a lover, a friend, a redhead, a kitty mommy, and an aspirer to The Nobel Peace Prize.

For nearly twenty years, her work with words has been instrumental in the spiritual lives of thousands of clients. She has received many accolades for her sermons, corporate speeches, and workshop presentations.

Dr. Corso is the founder of Sanctuary, an online spiritual community. She publishes a weekly e-newsletter, "Seeds for Sanctuary." She is the author of *The Peace Diet—The 44-Day Feast to Personal Peace*. Dr. Corso lives in New York City with her cat, Charles.

To contact the author, or to be added to the "Seeds for Sanctuary" list, kindly e-mail:
NYCSanctus@aol.com

Please visit the *God's Dictionary* pages on the Sanctuary website: www.sanctuarycommunity.org